The Secr
of the

The
Secret Places
of
the Shannon

JOHN M. FEEHAN

ROYAL CARBERY BOOKS

ROYAL CARBERY BOOKS
36 Beechwood Park, Ballinlough, Cork

Trade Distributors:
MERCIER PRESS
Douglas Village Cork

Trade enquiries to CMD DISTRIBUTION,
55a Spruce Avenue, Stillorgan Industrial Park, Blackrock, Dublin

© The Estate of John M Feehan

First published in 1980 under the title *The Magic of the Shannon*

ISBN 0 946645 09 4

DEDICATED TO
MARY AND BRENDAN SMITH
WHOSE UNFAILING HELP
MADE THIS BOOK POSSIBLE

Printed in Ireland by Colour Books Ltd.

INTRODUCTION

My last two books, *The Wind that Round the Fastnet Sweeps* and *The Magic of the Kerry Coast* were about the sea and my yacht *Dualla*. Alas I have become too old to face any more the pounding waves and the restless winds. I sold *Dualla* and parting with her after so many happy and adventurous years together was like as if some corner of my life left me for all time. But then I suppose all life is a series of goodbyes, each as painful in its own way as the one that went before it.

From the letters I received it seems as if quite a lot of people enjoyed my books about the sea, but a few complained that, despite the laughter and fun, they thought them too sad. They were, of course, thinking of those parts dealing with our tragic and painful history, but I have found it impossible to ignore these incidents. You cannot visit a place, say like Auschwitz, and write only about the goods in the souvenir shop, and every little village in Ireland was at one time or another almost a miniature Auschwitz. These things happened and we cannot change the past which is part and parcel of our race memories. The ordinary decent English tourists who come in thousands to this country every year have been kept in complete ignorance of what really happened and my experience is that they are all most anxious to search out the truth. A travel book which ignores this is, to say the least, incomplete. The majority of those English tourists, far from being offended, experience a deep sorrow that any of their rulers could have been so heartless and cruel and they have made a common bond with the Irish people who have responded by welcoming them, most sincerely. The best homage we ourselves can pay our brave ancestors is to try to make the Ireland they handed over to us at such gigantic sacrifice, a better place for everyone to live in, and to do this without rancour or bitterness.

A few have accused me of diverting at times into what they described as 'obscene'. That charge I must deny. What I have written is no more than the conversations anyone can hear in any pub or fireside in rural Ireland, earthy but not vulgar; erotic, perhaps, but not pornographic. Here I am reminded of the respectable lady who was complimenting Dr Samuel Johnson on the publication of his mamoth dictionary:

'I am delighted, Dr Johnson,' she said, 'that there are no dirty words in your dictionary.'

'Did you look for them, madam?' was Johnson's quick reply.

Some others have asked me if the stories I told were really true. I recorded them as I heard them and I never insulted any teller by questioning the accuracy of what he had to say. If I have misled my readers then I have been misled myself, but that does not worry me too much. To those who are ardently searching for truth perhaps a travel book is not the best source. I would recommend the *Summa Theologica* by St Thomas Aquinas in twenty volumes. I believe it can be bought on the hire purchase — and if that doesn't suit there is always the Penny Catechism.

This book is about the Shannon and it hasn't been an easy one to write for the simple reason that trying to describe the beauty of the Shannon is like trying to paint a soul. On and off over the years, I have cruised there on week-ends and short periods so there was nothing very new in taking a longer cruise. The boat I used was a thirty foot seamaster cruiser with two sleeping cabins, a main cabin, a refrigerator and, believe it or not, a shower. These luxuries I was not used to on *Dualla*. I hired her from Brendan Smith of *Silver Line Cruisers*, Banagher. Brendan is not only a man who hires boats but he is also a friend and I have dedicated this book to himself and his wife Mary as a little token of gratitude for all their kindness. At first I thought of buying a boat but when I went into the facts carefully I concluded that, unless you live close enough to the river or can travel there every weekend at least from April to October, it is cheaper and easier in the long run to hire. And there are several excellent hire companies with first class boats.

I found cruising the Shannon more reflective than cruising on the sea. I was less tense and less apprehensive about possible calamities and, therefore, much more relaxed. I filled several notebooks with the strangest reveries that sometimes peep out from the hidden retreats of the mind and maybe some day in the far distant future I might gather them together in another book. But I did notice that on the Shannon I was less concerned with the mystery of death than is my norm. I think that can be explained by an impish idea planted in my mind by an old grave-digger who spent his entire life delivering people to the other side. 'When the Last Day comes,' he explained, 'and when Gabriel blows the bugle for everyone to get up, nobody will be allowed into the Great Hall of Judgement until he first rubs out the lies on his headstone and writes in the truth instead. Supposing it said on an ould farmer's headstone that he was a good family man, when he wasn't, then on the Last Day he'd have to blot that out and write instead that he fathered three children in different parts of the parish and that no servant girl was safe in the house with him. Everyone will have to do the same.'

I must frankly admit that this idea has caused me some apprehension, but on the other hand it has taken a lot of the gloom out of death. It is consoling to know that most of one's friends will be quite busy on the Last Day. As a precaution however, I have begged my family not to compose too flattering an epitaph when I die, in case I might be unduly delayed in getting into the Great Hall. It would be safer, I have told them, to stick to the facts.

7

Well I hope you will enjoy this little book on the Shannon and that it may inspire you to spend a cruising holiday there. Believe me, there are very few holidays in any part of the world as good.

J. M. F.

January 1980

1

The year was 1944. The great European war of slaughter and destruction was coming to an end. Two young lovers stood on the rambling bridge at Killaloe listening to the whispering sounds of evening as the shadows of a dying autumn sunset fell across the gently-flowing Shannon. They had spent the hot afternoon strolling around this historic town of ivy-wreathed ruins. In the grounds of the old cathedral they had admired the superb Irish-Romanesque doorway with the carvings of little animals whose tails twisted into the hair of human heads as if to emphasise the unity of all living things. They read some of the solemn pompous tablets on the walls commemorating the colonels and brigadiers who built the empire in brutality and whose epitaphs tried to create the impression that heaven itself awaited their arrival with baited breath. Arm in arm they strolled through the old graveyard and studied the Redfield tomb, with its semi-comic carvings, which made one feel it was the work of a ninth century saint rather than a nineteenth century stonecutter with a magnificent sense of the ridiculous. Later they climbed to the top of the town and searched for Kincora, the legendary palace of the great Brian Boru. A man in his early fifties with greying hair – to them an old, old man – pointed out where it was, and said that long years after Brian's death the Connaughtmen raided the whole countryside, demolished the palace and threw it stone after stone into the River Shannon. There was nothing left now except a mound of clay that hid the forgotten dead. The glory of Kincora, the most beautiful palace in all Ireland, was gone and there was not even a plaque to commemorate its existence. 'That's the way of life,' the man had said. 'Here today, gone tomorrow. Everyone dies, everything is forgotten.' But they did not share his sad dejection. They were young and in love and would be married in a few weeks. The thorns of disappointment had not yet pierced their souls. The sorrow and pains of life were far away beyond the horizon they could not see. They knew nothing of the sadness beneath the surface. A world of hopes, dreams, boundless happiness was fondly holding out its welcoming arms, like a bright star in a far-off sky, and only the exquisite music of young love sang in their hearts as, hand-in-hand, they gazed over the parapet at the meandering swirling waters and the wondrous magic of the Shannon. It was one of those lovely moments in life when time blended with eternity and love seemed everlasting.

Thirty-five years later I returned to Killaloe. Little had changed — yet everything had changed. She was dead and I was now old and alone. Of the thousand promises that life held out to us on that far off evening only a few had been fulfilled. Youth had put too many dreams into our heads, foolish dreams where one walks among the stars and touches the infinite. I retraced our steps through the ancient ruins, the hilly winding streets, no longer searching for the palace but perhaps unconsciously searching for something else that had vanished as surely and as finally as the glories of Kincora. Yet I only found what I always find in these painful moments of contact with the past; that one cannot live weighed down by the burden of memories and that the only thing left to do is to go right on. With weary listless steps I made my way back to the pier where the cruiser was berthed. Under the latticed trees in the twilight, young couples were whispering words of love, locked in each others' arms, full of the joy of being alive and brimming with hope at the never-ending future of happiness they believe awaited them. On board I sat for a long time in the cockpit listening to the sad far-away sound of dance music floating across the water, gazing at the twinkling lights of the street-lamps, like threaded sparks, peeping through the trees. When the stars, from the frontiers of eternity, began to appear one by one in the night sky, I made my way down into the cabin, went to bed, and my bewildered thoughts faded away in a deep sleep.

> *There was a time when meadow, grove and stream*
> *The earth, and every common sight*
> *To me did seem*
> *Apparelled in celestial light,*
> *The glory and the freshness of a dream*
> *It is not now as it hath been of yore*
> *Turn whereso'er I may*
> *By night or day,*
> *The things which I have seen I now can see no more.*

Early next morning as the summer sun drifted lazily across a blue cloudless sky, I undid the warps and sailed away from Killaloe out into the shining waters of the great Lough Derg. Maxie, my Alsatian-husky dog, well known to readers of my two previous books *The Wind that Round the Fastnet Sweeps*, and *The Magic of the Kerry Coast*, sat on the forward deck surveying the scene around him and sniffing the air like an old sea pirate about to set off on a hunt for hidden treasure. The beautiful wooded shores swept in all their grandeur towards the devious edge of the water. There had been soft summer rain during the night and little rivulets ran down the slopes, like throbbing veins, bringing life to the parched valley of the Shannon. Now and again there were openings in the woods and I could see the purple heather and yellow whin climbing up the rugged hills. Those same hills of Clare have a mystical, elf-like quality all their own, so that you would almost expect fairies and leprechauns to dance and laugh and bounce from behind the knarled whitethorns and wave a friendly greeting at you as you passed. Indeed just to the west I could see standing out, Craglee Fort, which once was, and they tell me still is, the home of the fairy queen Aebhill. It was there she put Brian Merriman on trial and condemned him to several floggings with the cat-o-nine-tails because he refused to get married even though according to local women, he had all the necessary qualifications. Aebhill was the banshee of the Dalcassian clan, who warned Brian Boru that he would never return from the Battle of Clontarf, and whose wild wail could be heard piercing the surrounding hills whenever an O'Brien or an O'Kennedy died. They tell me, however, that she hasn't been seen much of late on account of technological progress in matters of death and she is supposed to have said herself at a recent wake near Tuamgraney: 'What with funeral parlours, morticians and luxury coffins you wouldn't know who a man was or whether he was alive or dead and maybe 'tis how you'd start crying for the wrong person altogether!'

As I sailed along past the beautiful Tinarana Bay I could see in the distance to the north-west the famous Pairc-na-nEach, or Field of the Horses, the site of Brian Boru's magnificent and extensive stables. That whole stretch of countryside from Killaloe to Scarriff was part of Brian's royal palace, which included not only his stables, but his military encampments and barracks; his detention quarters where upwards of one thousand hostages were kept in the comfort befitting their high station; as well as the farms, gardens, craftshops and everything pertaining to a major royal household. As I cruised along past this historic landscape my mind turned on the great Brian, his place in Irish history and his great gift in the leadership of men. In the history of every nation there is usually one outstanding personality whose greatness spans the centuries, defies the ravishment of time and outlives even death itself. In France it was Napoleon; in Germany Bismark; in America Lincoln. In our own country the choice would rest between Brian Boru and Michael Collins. When Brian's brother, Mahon, was murdered, Brian became King of Munster and he quickly set about breaking the power of the Danes, and subduing all the other Irish chieftains in his kingdom. The Danes had won most of their victories through their mastery of the art of naval warfare, an art virtually unknown to the Irish. Brian saw his own weakness and in a few years established

12

a navy of longships superior to the enemy. Using this navy, combined with first class land forces, he broke the power of the Danes in Munster, captured their headquarters on Scattery and cleared them from any outposts they had on Lough Derg. He next turned his attention to the wavering Irish chiefs and, moving on them one at a time, he took hostages and received their submission. Malachy was High King of Ireland in those days. He was a decent, honourable man but a weak, indecisive ruler. He did not seem to have anything like the calibre required to contain the Danes, to discipline the rebellious Irish chieftains, or to come to grips with the bands of armed robbers infesting the country. Outside of the Kingdom of Munster anarchy reigned. On the other hand Brian was a realist, who saw that there could be no lasting peace or prosperity in Ireland without a strong ruler and there was no reason why he himself should not be that ruler. Had he not shown all the qualities of a great leader in his government of Munster? It was this sense of realism, and not just vanity, that persuaded him to try his luck, but as there were no elections, proportional represent-ation or vote-touting in those days he had to seek the high-kingship by the only means available to him, namely force. By a series of well-timed threats, cajolings, flatteries, marriages, alliances, he finally made it clear to Malachy, and to all others, what he was after, and when he deemed the time ripe he marched his superb army towards Malachy's royal palace at Tara. Poor Malachy was taken unawares and in a gentlemanly way told Brian that he had not enough men to give battle and requested a month's delay in order that he might muster an army together. With great chivalry and gallantry Brian agreed and made camp peacefully at a discreet and respectable distance from Tara. Malachy then set about the task of forming an army. He tried his friends among the chieftains of Ulster and Cannaught but they, having shrewdly guessed what way the wind was blowing, refused help. At the end of the month with a sad and heavy heart Malachy made his way to Brian's tent, with only a few hundred horsemen, and told him that he regretted he was unable to raise an army and give battle and so he could only acknowledge defeat and hand over the high-kingship to Brian. There are many discussions and conversations of history that I would have like to have eavesdropped on but none so much as those two intriguing meetings between Malachy and Brian.

Brian now set about consolidating his rule over the whole of Ireland. He took hostages from all the chieftains as a pledge of their good conduct and as a guarantee that they would implement his social, political and cultural policies in their territories. He did not hesitate to execute the hostages, or blind their eyes out, if his directives were not obeyed. He perfected his army and was certainly the first Irish leader to have a competent navy of several hundred ships. He put an end to the running sore of violent robberies by executing the perpetrators one and all, even on suspicion, so that wrongdoers lived in constant fear of his drastic justice, while the ordinary people were able to live their lives in reasonable contentment. All over the country he began large scale rebuilding of monasteries and schools which had been burned or plundered by the Danes, and he was one of the first to inaugurate scholarships for promising students who wished to extend their studies at universities on the continent of Europe. All in all Ireland had never enjoyed such a period of peace and prosperity as those years when Brian was high-king. But the Danes decided they were going to have one last try. Ireland was too valuable a prize to let slip through their fingers. In Dublin they assembled a powerful army, drawn mainly from the Scandinavian countries, but before they had time to move into the heart of the country Brian routed them at Clontarf. He was then an old man of seventy-five and he remained in his tent throughout the combat. Towards evening when news was brought to him that the battle was won, but that his son and grandson were killed, he asked his attendants to leave him so that he could pray for their souls alone. He threw himself on his knees beside his rough camp bed sad and heartbroken, and remained there until near dusk when he was abruptly aroused by four Danes trying to escape under cover of twilight. They saw the old man and rushed upon him with drawn swords. In a matter of minutes it was over. Brian was dead, but it is a measure of the toughness of this aged warrior that he killed three of his assailants before he finally fell.

Brian's county, Clare, is one of the many Irish counties where folk tradition is a living vigorous thing. When you leave the tourist resorts, the luxury restaurants, and go deeper into the country, where every little field is a masterpiece, you will find history and tradition in every crag, character in every profile and poetry in every soul. I once met an old man in east Clare, so old that he seemed dead until he moved, who spoke about Brian Boru as if he lived in the recent past and not one thousand years ago. 'He was a smart man, be all accounts,' he said, 'for he put the country on its feet again and the fear of God into every robber. He didn't have much of a run of luck with his wives who were a contrary lot. I heard the ould people for to say that their kisses never went farther than their lips and tasted like the honey of a wasp. But he wasn't short of a bit of fun, all the same, for he had hundreds of tally women around the place, and small blame to him. A person's entitled to a bit of diversion now and again, especially when you have no radio or T.V. By all accounts he was a fine looking man, big and handsome, and 'tis said he wore the tallest hat goin' to Mass on a Sunday. He had the biggest eatin' house in all Ireland, with more than a hundred servants dishin' up the best of Danish beer and Irish whiskey, and I often heard tell of the singing, shouting and dancing that went on at all them feasts, and 'tis said the leprechauns and fairies used to join them in the small hours of the morning when things would be slowin' down a bit.' Although the harsh imprint of time was showing on his face there was a merry twinkle in his eye as he continued: 'When all the devilment was over Brian and his companions would go to the abbey on Holy Island, near Mountshannon, for to go to confession, do penance and cure their sick heads.

15

Brian's brother was abbot there, don't you see, so he could make things easy and could get the community to pray while Brian recuperated. Ah, them were the days,' he concluded sadly. 'There isn't the likes of them to be had anywhere now. Poor Brian is gone, God rest him, and so is Kincora, and the devil a bit is left now only the stories you'd hear the ould people tellin' around the fire of a winter's evening if the wireless was broke, and you wouldn't know in the hell whether them stories is true or lies, for if you get the name of an early riser you can sleep until dinnertime. But sure I suppose it don't matter anyway, when you're dead you're dead, and there's no use boilin' the cabbage twice. Brian is dead and gone and 'tis as well for us let the poor man rest in peace. May the Lord have mercy on his soul and on all the souls of the faithful departed.'

> *Oh, where Kincora, is Brian the Great?*
> *And where is the beauty that once was thine?*
> *Oh, where are the princes and nobles that sate*
> *At the feast in thy halls and drank the red wine?*

I had now passed between the verdant Scilly Island and the Lushing Rocks and came into what can be the roughest part of the lake. But today everything was calm with scarcely a ripple on the surface. Summer had come and a loving sun was sharing its heat with hills and valleys and kissing back to life the sleeping beauty of the earth. The friendly sheen of morning was creeping over the tranquil lake. In the distance I could see the little islands of solitude which dot the entrance to Mountshannon harbour where I would make my first call. There was no other boat on the lake. I suppose it is in such moments of supreme beauty and peace a man begins to suspect that those deep yearnings he feels to 'get away from it all' are but the voice of a well of tranquillity within the soul trying to blend and merge with the tranquillity of the universe — for are we not all one: earth, sea and sky — all creatures of the one God. It must have been such moments that wrung from the tormented

16

soul of Keats the plaintive cry:

> *O aching time! Oh moments big as years!*
> *All as ye pass, swell out the monstrous truth.*
> *And press it so upon our weary griefs*
> *That unbelief has not a space to breath.*

Lough Derg is the largest of the Shannon lakes and many believe it to be the most beautiful also, with its enchanting variety of wooded isles, rocky bays, tree-lined shores, fringing the undimmed beauty of the hills of Clare. And as I drew near Mountshannon, it looked its loveliest, so that one could never imagine the savage storms that sometimes whip it up into a wild mass of breaking water. Slowly I guided the cruiser between Cribby and Bushy Islands, those two little retreats where happy wild things play unhurt by man, and made fast near the end of the sheltered pier. The harbour was crowded; German, French, Belgian, Dutch — but no Irish! We have yet to discover the beauty on our own doorstep.

Out on deck, in the glorious sunshine, I had a light lunch and afterwards strolled along the pier towards Mountshannon. To get to the village itself you walk up a delightful little laneway under an archway of trees where the tops lean over as if bent in prayer. While I meandered along this peaceful path Maxie was frolicking to his heart's content chasing the butterflies as they glided in and out through the quivering sunbeams. From beneath the rich foliage bluebells, primroses and foxgloves peeped out and opened their petals to the foraging bees. A nearby garden was aflame with flowers of every colour, overlooked from a hillock by a magnificent tree of cherry blossoms just about to lose its bridal veil. Although Mountshannon's tree-lined street is spotlessly clean and tidy, it hasn't lost its old-world atmosphere, and its intriguing mixture of Georgian, Tudor and Scottish architecture is always a joy to behold. Mountshannon was famous in the early eighteenth century for its fairs, but because there was so much street fighting and bloodshed it had its licence transferred to Whitegate, where,

17

it is said, 'peace reigned'. Maybe the cause of all the fighting was that in this small village of one hundred souls there were Catholics, Protestants, Methodists and Baptists, each with their own place of worship and their own preacher thundering fire and brimstone from the altar. I strolled around for about half an hour and returned to the pier through a kind of miniature nature trail by the edge of the lake, tastefully laid out and maintained, with a splendid view of the historic isle of Iniscealtra which is less than a mile across the bay.

I yielded to a sudden impulse to visit the island and so when I got back to the pier I launched the punt and outboard and motored across the sound. As I neared the little boat-slip Maxie, who seemed over-eager to land, jumped too soon, missed the slip and splashed into the water; but he quickly swam ashore, shook himself and rolled over and over in the grass with obvious glee. Holy Island or Iniscealtra, is where Brian Boru and his friends came when they wanted a physical dry out and a spiritual Turkish bath, and indeed there must be few places in the whole lake more pleasant. On this lightly-wooded island there are five churches, a large graveyard, a hermit's cell and an unfinished round tower. The wattle huts where the monks lived have long since vanished without trace. Some of these must have been fairly grim if we are to judge from an early manuscript account of one, MacCreiche; he lived in a cell with 'a stone at his back, a stone at each of his sides, and a stone at his face. There MacCreiche began to keep Lent for fear and terror of Hell'. Strange, it was' fear and terror, and not love of God that made him do this. Yet as you stroll around the old ruins, lassoed with ivy and greyed to the eves by wind and rain, you cannot help feeling close to the eternal. If you let the imagination run free you can almost hear, coming out of the past, the murmur of prayer mingling with the music of the singing birds in every tree. The quiet gentleness of the green grass and the beauty of the flowing sunlight seemed today to fill all the island with the presence of God. As I slowly wandered through the graves of those men who knew and loved immortal things, my thoughts were naturally close to the mystery of death. Here they rested in their hundreds, lulled by the gentle waters of the Shannon, after more than a thousand years, all their hopes, joys, worries and sadnesses at an end.

> *Leaves have their time to fall*
> *And flowers to wither at the north wind's breath*
> *And stars to set — but all,*
> *Thou hast all season for thine own,*
> *Oh Death!*

Every community of saints had its delightful eccentric and Iniscealtra was not wanting. One of them, by the name of Coscrach, had his headstone inscribed with his footprint! There is another strange grave with an inscription 'Nad I Dechenboir' — The Grave of Ten Men. Who were the ten, and why were they buried together? What story of romance or tragedy lies behind that mound of earth? One of the earliest references to Iniscealtra is contained in the journal of an English traveller, Dyneley, in 1680:

> Iniscealtra. This is two small miles about in the Shannon River... called the Seven Churches of Asia. Here once a year the superstitious Irish go to do penance, and are enjoined to walk around barefooted seven times, and they who fear hurting their feet may hire others to do it for them!

I love that bit about hiring others to do your penance for you. The rich we shall always have with us. These pilgrimages survived into modern times but because the younger pilgrims, it appears, took off more than their shoes, the outings were suppressed by the clergy at the turn of the century. Inside one of the churches on Iniscealtra, The Church of the Wounded, tradition holds that a woman could not conceive. The unseemly scramble for discreet position in this ruin on holidays of obligation made ecclesiastical action necessary and all pilgrimages were finally suppressed. Suppression became the weapon of the ecclesiastics over the last century, but the monks of old understood the frailties of human nature much better and they were always ready to try to heal them with a touch of wisdom and discretion. I spent more than an hour on the island just wandering aimlessly around, thinking, musing, contemplating, and as the first shades of evening appeared, I launched the punt and made my way back to the pier at Mountshannon. On board again I let go the warps and motored out into the lake now towards Scarriff harbour where I was going to spend the night and meet two friends who would join me cruising for the next few days. The trip up to Scarriff is a short one — a matter of two hours or so. I sailed out between Bushy and Cribby Islands once again in order to avoid the many unmarked rocks on the northern shore, and then turned to starboard leaving to port the red buoys that mark the dangerous middle-ground shoal. As I passed Holy Island the new perspective from the lake was most impressive. There is no doubt that these old monks knew how to pick a good spot; well sheltered, rich fertile land, good fishing and protected by a natural moat of water. Further on I passed the ruins of Cahir Castle and remembered the many romantic and adventurous stories told about its past. It was a very famous poteen still and was so well defended that the police were afraid to come near it. On one occasion a Scarriff woman was on a pilgrimage to Holy Island and on the way back she called in for a drop of the stuff for her husband who had a bad dose of 'flu. They filled a pint bottle for her but when she landed in Scarriff the police were waiting and found the bottle in her bag. 'What's in that bottle?' the sergeant asked. 'Ah now, sergeant,' replied the woman. 'As true as God is over me 'tis only a drop of blessed water from the well at Iniscealtra that I'm bringing home to ease me sick husband.' 'That's not holy water,' said the sergeant who had just tasted it. 'See for yourself.' The woman put a drop on her tongue and stood transfixed with her eyes turned up towards heaven. 'A miracle! A miracle!' she screamed at the top of her voice. 'Thank you God! Thank you God!' and away she ran up the village clutching her bottle leaving the police standing in bewilderment. When they recovered their senses and located her house they found the bottle alright, but it was now full of holy water. The still continued to flourish until the government sent a detachment of soldiers, with two pieces of artillery, who levelled it to the ground and put an end to its lucrative activities.

It is not easy to pick out the entrance to the Scarriff River at any time as there are many similar openings in the reed-banks, but it is particularly difficult in a setting sun — the glare makes the buoys almost impossible to see. However, there is a very prominent new bungalow and a group of white houses on the hill near the entrance and by steering in this general direction it is possible to pick out the buoys in good time. When I reached the entrance I reduced speed in case I went aground or came too close to one of the banks, so that I was barely gliding along through the tall reeds which looked as if they were gossiping with each other. The gentleness of evening was creeping over the earth. The tidy farms, the rolling hills, the hawthorn hedges, the singing birds, the flocks of sheep and cattle silently grazing, gave a kind of a wandering pensive air to the whole countryside. This is the land of poets who poured out their hearts and souls in song:

The heart would lighten when worn with troubles
Weakened and weary or filled with sufferings
In a little wretch lacking both riches and land,
If over the tops of the wood he'd glance
At ducks in flocks in a mist-free haven
With the swan in their midst along with them sailing,
The fish with jollity jumping high;
Attractive and speckled, a perch in sight
The hue of the lake and the blue of the waves,
That strongly, heavily, noisily came.
The birds in the trees were merry and joyous
The doe in the woodlands leaping beside me
The hunthorn sounding and hosts in sight
Beagles chasing and reynard in flight.

21

These lines were written by one of the greatest of Irish poets, Brian Merriman, and I was now sailing through the heart of Merriman country. Merriman's erotic and rabelaisian poem, *The Midnight Court*, is rightly regarded as by far the most important contribution to Irish literature in the eighteenth century. The richness of language, the astonishing vocabulary of words with all their subtleties and shades of meaning, the courage shown in handling the subject, have ensured for this poem an enduring and lasting greatness. Its theme is the Irishwoman's right to sex and marriage and the Irishman's inclination to consider the former but to avoid the latter at all costs. It takes the form of a court case tried at midnight in one of the wild glens quite close to where I was now passing. Aebhill, queen of the fairies, is the judge and the poem begins with a young girl giving evidence as to all her fruitless attempts to get a man to marry. Her description of her own physical beauty leaves little to the imagination:

Look at my waist! How slender my frame!
I'm not scraggy or bent or lame:
Head, feet and figure that I'm not ashamed of:
And the choicest of girths to satisfy males with.

She has tried every known ruse, including witchcraft, to capture a bedfellow but all to no avail. She is followed in the witness-box by a little old man who attacks her viciously as a whore and a lazy slut who is only looking for someone to support her in idleness and to take her away from the dirt in which she was reared:

You've nothing to boast in your ugly past
But useless louts, men of scraps and bags
We know the cringer who was your father,
Without friend, reputation, bed or a farthing.

He extends his attacks to all the women of Ireland as nothing but a race of trollops trying to ensnare decent hardworking men. As an example he cites his own personal case where he recently married a young girl, full of purity and

22

innocence, as he thought, only to find out on the wedding night that she was well pregnant by another man:

> *It wasn't frivolous gossip or lying chatter,*
> *Or woman-tells-woman-it type of yarn,*
> *But the deed spoke out with truth and maturity*
> *And she presented a son to me prematurely.*

He then lashed out at the whole institution of marriage, called for its abolition and demanded freedom for the men and women of Ireland to fornicate to their hearts content in the ditches, hedges and haybarns of the country. But the young girl does not let him away with it all that easily. She jumps back into the witness box and tells the court exactly what went wrong in this fellow's marriage. The young bride-to-be was looking forward to a night of fun but when she got him in bed she found he could do absolutely nothing. She tried every known trick, technique and aphrodisiac to arouse him, but to no avail, so why should she not love elsewhere?

> *But she would stretch out luxuriantly*
> *Bit by bit his thoughts seducing*
> *Side by side and her limbs around him*
> *Mouth on mouth pawing him downwards.*
> *Often around him she twined her foot*
> *From his belt to his knee her brush she rubbed*
> *She snatched from his loins the quilt and the blanket*
> *With a cheerless old heap to play and dally*
> *It's often she grasped his lifeless sceptre*
> *And rubbed its mouth to her groin with frenzy*
> *Took it within her soft hand nimbly,*
> *And roused not the wretch to excitement or business.*

The young girl ends her harange by launching a ferocious attack on the celibacy of the clergy and on the rule which prevents them from getting married. She states in no uncertain manner that they are human like the rest of us, and have indeed fathered numerous illegitimate children throughout the country. These remarks stung the Irish clergy of many generations to the quick for in 1946, more than a hundred years after Merriman's death, a committee got together to put up a memorial to him in Feakle grave-yard, close to Scarriff, but so strong was the opposition of the clergy that they succeeded in preventing it, even though the President of Ireland, Sean T. O'Kelly, and the Taoiseach, Eamon de Valera, were actively supporting the project.

Brian Merriman was born in 1750. His father was a stonemason from Clare and his mother was a small farmer's daughter from south Galway. When he was young the family moved to Killeany, not too far from Scarriff, and it was here in this wild mountainous county he was reared. He was educated at a hedge school and became quite a brilliant linguist and mathematician and when he was grown up he started his own hedge school in Killeany. Having written *The Midnight Court*, things became a little hot for him in the country so he transferred to Limerick city where he started a private school. He married Kate Collins and they had two daughters, both of whom married tailors and emigrated to London. Brian died, rather suddenly on the streets of Limerick in 1805. The manuscript of *The Midnight Court* was not published until about 1850 but numerous copies, transcribed in copper-plate writing, were in circulation throughout the country. The edition which I would recommend, not only to every Irishman and woman, but to every visitor to the country who wants to understand rural Ireland, is a paperback called *The Midnight Court* translated by Patrick C. Power, from which I have taken the foregoing quotations. This is a dual-languge book with the Irish on the left hand pages and the English on the opposite pages. It is a particularly interesting edition because it contains seventy-five lines which are absent from other editions. It was quite understandable that these lines should be omitted in the past since, by naming certain people and their misdemeanours, they could be held to be grossly libellous. Dr Power not only brings his great scholarship to bear on this translation, but presents it in a most readable and acceptable form, and for those who understand Irish it is intriguing to compare both versions side by side.

Having made my way slowly up the meandering, winding river, where indeed at times I thought I had gone astray, I finally reached Scarriff pier where I was glad to see only two other cruisers berthed. Although there is ample room in the little harbour for several boats there are not enough bollards, and in crowded conditions one is very often forced to tie up to young trees, litter bins or any other fixed object one can find. When I made fast, Maxie jumped ashore with the excited air of one expecting some great adventure. All the way up the narrow Scarriff river he had seen dogs, cattle and donkeys along the banks and he eyed them with a mixture of wild desire on the one hand, and fear of jumping on the other. This was strange and new to him because, although he had cruised a lot in the past, it was nearly always out at sea where there were no banks and nothing visible except the odd seagull. I took him for a short five minute stroll through the scrub and having barked once or twice at a few cows and donkeys who just looked stupidly at him, he gave it up and philosophically accepted their right to be alive and well. Back on board I went down below for a short nap while the dinner was cooking and later, when the meal was over, I sat out on deck with a mug of coffee enjoying the beauty and peace of this secret, land-locked harbour, and letting my mind wander along the byways of memory.

Scarriff is both an unusual and intriguing village. It is the capital of the wild, hilly, gnarled countryside of east Clare, a land of goblins, ghosts, fairies and banshees. It is a village that never lost its character or never sold its soul. Modernisation has been accepted as a necessary mischief, but it has been kept securely in its place. It is a village of singers, storytellers, musicians, imaginative, exciting personalities, and it attracts a wide variety of visitors. In the summertime you could meet ambassadors, ministers, bankers, royalty, tinkers, cobblers, farmers, labourers on holiday there or just passing through. Every face you see in Scarriff can be a new surprise opening up new and astonishing worlds.

This little village has a very special place in the archives of my memory because it was here, many years ago, I got to know one of the most unusual human beings I ever came across. I have always found something delightful about those accidental friendships that sometimes end in the discovery of a strange and original soul. I think it is the *Readers Digest* who run a series of articles under the general heading of *The Most Unforgetable Character I Ever Met*. If I were contributing to this series, a girl from the north country whom I met in Scarriff, would be the subject of my composition. She was young. She was beautiful. She was intelligent. She was cultured. After our first drink we were discussing obscurity in modern poetry. After our second drink she talked about the influence of Rabelais and Villon on Brian Merriman. She spoke so brilliantly on literary topics that I came to the conclusion she was a gifted teacher or university lecturer. But after our third drink she confided in me, with disarming candour, that she was a courtesan. She felt no embarrassment or inhibition whatever about her profession. Neither did I, so we were able to exchange freely those little professional anecdotes and confidences that people do when the drink loosens the tongue and conversation becomes slightly blurred. In her own way she had come to terms with the theology of her profession and spoke quite convincingly of her having chosen the better part. The majority of Irish women, she told me, had decided to sell their bodies while already in their teens. Their overpowering ambition was to find a man who would be their slave, support them, and satisfy their animal breeding instincts. In return for that they were prepared to give him the pleasurable use of their bodies at certain times, and decorate themselves at his expense so that he could show them off on social occasions like prize poodles. The sole topic of conversation amongst unmarried girls was men, marriage, security and breeding. When they had hunted down their man and browbeaten him with promises and tears, they got him to marry. The only difference between

26

them and the professional courtesan was that the professional is paid by time while the married woman is paid by contract. The commodity they have for sale is, in both cases, the same. As she was speaking and unfolding her ideas the publishing spark in me saw what a wonderful book she could write, so despite the alcoholic and fuzzy thinking I put this idea to her. Perhaps I should say honestly at this point that the other commodity she had on offer, besides a potential book, was far away beyond my financial means. So having discussed that matter and disposed of it in the friendliest possible way, we understood each other clearly from the start. No, she said. A book would be out of the question. It would expose her techniques and her ingenious method of acquiring customers, and by revealing too much could destroy what she had so carefully and successfully evolved. She began her career on the beat in English hotels, she explained, attending to the needs of middle-aged executive and professional men who, for the most part, were impotent from over-eating and tension before they had even reached the age of forty. They were not deeply interested in sex itself and what they seemed to need most was somebody to listen to their boring conversation and give them a massage while doing so. These unfortunate men, she said, are dead long before they really die. The whole thing was boring except for the occasional laugh, such as the wealthy business man who only wanted to play push-penny stark naked around the floor, or a distinguished manufacturer who, having stripped himself, and with her in the nude, then just sang hymns from a hymnal for half-an-hour. She got a bit tired of all this, she said, and for a while gave it up and worked in a pornographic bakery run by a friend. Then one day she read a short story by Guy de Maupassant about a prostitute in Paris who kept off the usual beats and concentrated on graveyards. This started the idea in her head that she should return to Ireland and try out what her French colleague had done so successfully in Paris. Displaying an extraordinary business acumen and insight, she developed this novel idea, which was never

27

tried before in this country. She would stroll around the graves in a large Irish city, dressed in widow's black, pretending to be in mourning, until she saw somewhere a recently bereaved husband praying or putting flowers on his wife's grave. She would then move over near where he was, sob a little at some other grave creating the impression that it was her dead husband's, and then pretend to faint. He would come to her assistance and from there on it was child's play. Widowers, she confided in me, sometimes have scruples about going to bed with another woman because they feel they might be letting their dead wives down, but they have no such scruples about going to bed with a recently bereaved widow — two sets of scruples cancel each other out. With skilful manipulation she could knock £1,000 in cash or in kind from a man in a month. Then she dropped him when he was beginning to expect things for nothing, changed graveyards and moved on to the next conquest. 'It is a highly lucrative business,' she explained. 'And you can see why I could never write the book you ask. It would blow the lid off the whole thing and destroy overnight what I have so carefully built up through the years.'

Many years later the story had an unexpected sequel. I was at a funeral in one of the city graveyards and, when the obsequies were over, I wandered alone through the hundreds of lonely neglected graves, those grim memorials to man's indifference and forgetfulness. It was a dull, cloudy day, oppressive and sad. As I wandered aimlessly through the rows of grey headstones I suddenly saw her. She was on her knees, dressed in black, weeding a recent grave. I watched unseen for a while until I was certain it was her. It was easy to recognise her by her aristocratic features and wealth of jet-black hair. I was puzzled a little that I could see no prospective customer around. Then I walked slowly towards where she was kneeling and stopped. She looked up suddenly and an angry wave swept across her face.

'Go away,' she snapped rudely.

'Do you remember me?' I asked.

'How can I remember you all?' she answered with a trace

of bitterness in her voice. 'You are a vain lot of clowns to expect to be remembered as if each one of you was God's gift to women. Go away! I am no longer interested.'

'Do you not remember a pleasant summer's evening in Scarriff many years ago when I asked you to write a book?' I spoke calmly. She stood up and a beautiful smile came quickly over her face.

'Yes of course I do,' she said. 'I'm sorry, very sorry, for being so nasty just now. I thought you were an ex-customer. I'm so glad to see you again. But what are you doing here?'

I told her I just happened to be there, at a funeral, and with my usual sombre interest in the dead, I was strolling around when I spotted her. She seemed quite pleased to see me. She anticipated the question that was forming in my mind and explained that this was her husband's grave. He was five months dead. Yes, she had married despite all the harsh things she thought about marriage. About a year after we met in Scarriff she fell in love with one of her customers. He was only a few months a widower when they met at this very grave and it was love almost at first sight. For reasons of respectability they didn't get married until after his wife's first anniversary. I was curious to know what kind of a man she could fall in love with, so I remarked, very casually, that he must have been a remarkable person.

'Yes indeed he was,' she said winsomely. 'He was a most religious man, and he brought me back to my faith. As well, he was intelligent and widely read. He wrote a little poetry and was quite a good artist. Most important of all he never did or said a thing to hurt me.'

They went to Rome on their honeymoon and those days of spiritual upliftment and sensuality were the happiest of her life. Sadly they were only two years married when he died suddenly. He was a wealthy man and he had left her very well off. She had ordered a magnificent headstone, commemorating himself and his first wife, and she hoped it would be ready and in position shortly. As she was speaking the possibility of her writing the book came back into my mind and I gently broached the question to her. 'No,' she

29

said firmly. 'The past is gone and I don't want to re-live it all again. It would be too painful for me to remember all the people I betrayed and let down. Adultery is a very lonely business. It's all behind me now.' I could not help thinking how striking the change in her was since I first met her. As if she read my thoughts she said. 'I suppose you're surprised at all this change in me, but a man like you, so deeply interested in psychology, must surely know that no matter what a woman says, she wants above all, a home, a man to love and a God. I've had all three of them and it was wonderful. I never understood who or what I was until I met someone who loved me.' There was a moment's silence as her words sank in. Then, embarrassed, I made a move to go. At that she took off her gardening glove and smilingly gave me her hand. 'Good-bye,' she said. 'And I hope we will meet again, but not in a graveyard.'

'I hope so,' I replied. 'Perhaps it may be in Scarriff!'

The tranquil setting sun had clothed the hills of Clare in a garment of lavish colour; gold, yellow, copper and saffron, now slowly fading and blending into a magical twilight. As the stars began to come out and twinkle one by one, Maxie and myself made our way through the half shadows, along the rambling laneway which led to Scarriff. We crossed a rustic bridge and climbed a hill to the village square dominated by an old market-house from a bygone age. The street lamps had just come on. Little children were playing a last game of hop-scotch before going to bed, their happy faces unaware of how sad the world really is. Teenage visitors walked around the street, wearing dirty clothes to draw attention to themselves. From many pubs came the sound of music, song and laughter, but I felt there was a strange note of melancholy in the air and I did not join. I just strolled around the village and back down the laneway to the quiet little pier. There was a haunting sadness about the night, tender and beautiful, undefinable, like death, full of awe and reverence that penetrated the soul. The words of the psalmist crossed my mind: *In the evening weeping shall have place; in the morning gladness.* And so I went to bed, confident that the inspired tidings would be fulfilled, and that morning would bring the promised gladness. Maxie coiled up at the foot of my bunk gloriously indifferent to my gloomy moods and thoughts.

2

I was up early next morning and shortly after breakfast the two companions I was expecting arrived. I was delighted to have them with me. Cruising alone sounds very romantic but there are times when it can be awkward and difficult, especially on entering or leaving crowded harbours or locks. Both my friends were experienced men of boats, so there was no need for me to feel in any way worried or apprehensive so long as they were with me. Even more important still, they were men of a tranquil, pleasant and good humoured disposition. There are few things more disagreeable within the confines of a small boat than moody, sulky, cantankerous companions, the kind of people who lose their precious tempers and lash out at others when things don't go their way. In the cramped conditions of a small boat there can be no room for such unadaptable individuals. But today I had the best of companions with me, and as we moved down the Scarriff river they took over the boat so I sat out on the foredeck, supported by plenty of cushions, Maxie by my side, and enjoyed the cool, fresh breath of this lovely summer's morning. We sailed out into the lake and set our course for Garrykennedy which was about a two hour journey away. It was a magnificent summer's day with the gentlest of winds blowing from the south-west, and the whole countryside became a delicate landscape that could have inspired a Constable or a Turner. The tops of the distant mountains were hidden in veils of shimmering mist; the beautiful rays of the morning sun was bringing life to land and water; the clear blue sky was touched here and there by little fairy wisps of clouds. Everything seemed to bubble over with life and it was easy to understand how such a scene delighted the heart of Merriman:

> Do ghealfadh an croí a bhí crion le cianta
> Caite gan bhrí no líonta i bpianta
> An seithleach searbh gan sealbh gan seibhreas
> D'feachfadh tamall thar bharra na gcoillte.

On every side of me the prosperous little farmhouses of Clare, with their simple thatched hay-stacks, reeks of black-brown turf and patchwork fields, dotted the landscape and it was hard to imagine that not so very long ago this countryside, now smiling on all sides, saw the most terrible suffering, famine, evictions and death in the history of the nation, at the hands of particularly brutal landlords. With scant mercy they evicted the old, the sick, the feeble, the helpless little children most of whom died in their thousands by the roadside. On the roadsides of Clare there were no wounded, only the dead. One contemporary writer describes what it was like:

> Sixteen houses containing twenty-one families have been levelled in one village... As soon as one horde of house-less and all but naked paupers are dead, another whole-sale eviction doubles the number... As cabins became fewer lodgings became more difficult to obtain and the helpless creatures betake themselves to the nearest bog or ditch with their little children and thus huddled they die of disease and starvation.

One of these landlords boasted that he would 'whip Ireland into a tame cat'. Shortly afterwards he died and was buried with great pomp and ceremony. When his coffin was lowered into the grave the ragged Irish emerged stealthily from amongst the shrubbery and flung hordes of dead cats into his grave. It was the only way they could protest. Another, in 1870, who arrogantly tried to have a statue erected to himself in a public place, gave up the project when he heard that it would be blown up immediately it was unveilled.

Perhaps the most hated of all English monarchs in Ireland was Victoria, better known as the Famine Queen. Four million people were evicted during her reign, and alone in the three terrible years after the famine she permitted the eviction of some two hundred and sixty thousand human beings most of whom died of starvation. They say in Clare that if hell were a barrel and you lifted the lid off, the first person you would see roasting inside would be Victoria. Her dark memory still lives on in the folk culture of the people who coined for her the name 'Evictoria'. 'The bloody oul bitch,' a Clare famer once said to me. 'She starved millions to death and when she was dyin' herself she was such a prude that she gave orders for to leave her knickers on when she was being washed and what's more, she left instructions that the women who would be washing her was to be blindfolded.' But those days are gone, the landlords are gone, their magnificent mansions crumbling and decaying, their pompous tombstones covered in moss and lichen. The people they tried to crush and exterminate lived to see the last of them vanquished. Today the farmers of Clare can grow and prosper in security and peace, and rear their families without fear of hunger. Generation upon generation struggled on, despite being clubbed into insensibility time and time again, until our own day saw at last the end of the road. 'If I had my way,' the late Sir Winston Churchill is reported to have said to the painter Augustus John, 'I would exterminate the whole Irish race.' Sir Winston is gone, and the imperialism that he dedicated his life to is but a memory, yet the Irish race remains. The victory of good over evil is not only found in fairy tales but sometimes in real life too.

As we sailed along over the gleaming waters of Lough Derg the day became more and more awake. The woods, the islands, the shores seemed to become more beautiful bit by bit. Wild birds of the lake ventured out over the surface as if answering some strange primeval call to the fullness

33

and joy of life. There was an air of cheerfulness and hope everywhere as if the world were being re-born. In such ecstatic moments it was great to be alive and it was easy to believe in God.

It was high noon when we arrived at Garrykennedy. We tied up at the tiny western harbour in the shadow of an old castle. This was once an O'Kennedy stronghold and a neighbouring tribe, the Keoghs, cast anxious eyes on the rich O'Kennedy's islands. Unexpectedly they attacked, surprised the chieftain Brian and killed him — by no means an unusual event in those far off days. But Brian had a few handy sons and grandsons who were not willing to let such things pass unnoticed. They paid a suprise visit to the Keoghs, executed fifteen of them, and made the journey home with hundreds of their cattle. A fair warning to all others not to trifle with descendants of Brian Boru! Garrykennedy is a tiny harbour with room only for a few boats and in any kind of crowded conditions there can be some difficulty getting in and out. The pier itself is constructed of very rough stone, taken from the castle, which goes to show that disrespect for national monuments is not something peculiar to the present day. A sort of a new harbour has been created here but it is not deep enough for cruisers so one cannot help asking the question—why build a pier if boats cannot tie up alongside? After a cup of coffee we went for a stroll around the tastefully laid out parkland, Maxie delighted to be on dry land once more. Local tradition has it that on the site of this little park a famous incident took place in the thirteenth century which had far-reaching consequences for Ireland. The English Pope, Adrian IV, sent a cardinal over to Ireland on a tour of inspection since he wanted to collect enough evidence on the barbaric Irish to justify handing over the country to the King of England, Henry II. The cardinal's baggage was carried by over forty mules and asses, and on his way from Lohrra to Killaloe he made a detour around the lake to view the beautiful scenery and camped overnight here in Garrykennedy. While the sacred party were sound asleep the locals stole all the mules and asses and left the portly cardinal and his entourage with only their feet to carry them to Killaloe. Back in Rome the cardinal reported this to Adrian who is supposed to have angrily said: 'I must do something at once to convert these savage Irish,' whereupon he issued his famous Bull handing Ireland over to England. Incidentally, Adrian was a cousin of Henry II, and as they say in Tipperary, 'Cousins are useful betimes.'

Back again on board we had some difficulty in manoeuvring our way out of the little harbour because a number of other boats had come in while we were strolling around the village, but with that co-operative and friendly attitude one finds among all Shannon boatmen we were helped out of our difficulties and in no time on our way to our next port of call, Dromineer, which is but a short hour's run from Garrykennedy. This is a very richly wooded and luxuriant part of the lake which probably accounts for the high proportion of ascendency houses located in most scenic positions. There was a time when the ascendency were firmly in the saddle of public affairs and looked down upon the Irish as lackeys and stable-boys. Although born in Ireland their loyalties were to the British crown, and they gave unquestioning service in building the empire and crushing minorities wherever the interests of that crown demanded. They were the brigadiers, generals, colonels and majors of the last century, men of impeccable ignorance, but with the advent of Irish freedom their days of supremacy and influence came to an end. They then retreated into themselves, a sad decaying lot, who became figures of fun and objects of caricature. They drank the royal health on birthdays. They put their flags at half-mast on the lawns when some old warrior from one of the regiments died; indeed one, who had an ex-bugler as a valet, was known to have the last post sounded on his lawn on such sombre occasions. They bemoaned the good old days when the sun never set on the empire, and they were the empire's loyal servants. But however ludicrous or stupid they seemed to be, they were a thoroughly decent lot. Most of their lands

35

sloped down to the lakeside leaving them the owners of considerable stretches of foreshore. They rarely objected to any fisherman landing on their beaches to boil a pot of tea for a midday meal or afternoon snack; indeed they might very well invite such a visitor to the house for a little drink to warm him up after the day. Wherever or whenever they could help strangers or tourists in any way they did so, and were always ready for a friendly chat or exchange of views. Sadly, they are now being replaced by a totally different breed, mostly continentals, sour and hostile, locally known as 'the concentration-camp landlords'. This is because many have surrounded themselves with masses of barbed-wire fences. No more may the weary fisherman land where he likes to heat up his brew or take a well-earned rest.

To get into Dromineer harbour one must exercise a little caution as it is not quite as straightforward as it seems. If you keep too close to the southern side you run the risk of going aground on the many invisible rocks that dot this shoreline. But if you keep too far over to the other side there is the possibility that you will hit the underwater shoal running out from Goose Island. The best thing is to keep well off the southern shore and steer for the outer end of the pier but on no account go too close to Goose Island. These simple directions we followed and just one hour after leaving Garrykennedy we were safely tied up in Dromineer harbour in the shadow of the ruined castle that looked down on us, silent, beautiful, alone. There were a few other cruisers berthed alongside the pier, some with their lines of washed flimsies drying in the sun, in no way a source of temptation to the happy youngsters who splashed and swashed in rowing boats and other smaller craft, enjoying the cheerful sunshine of youth. We had a pleasant lunch out on deck but I think the wine made us languid, drowsy and comfortable, and on the principle that to enjoy ourselves today is much easier than to enjoy ourselves tomorrow, we decided to stay put in Dromineer until the following morning; so, propped up by various cushions, we lay back on deck balming in the calm restful air and lulled by the murmuring, healing sounds of summer, and feeling 'how very sweet it was to look into the fair and open face of heaven.'

A little more than an hour later my companions bestired themselves and decided to take the punt and go fishing around Urra Bay for the afternoon, while I opted for a long walk with Maxie to explore those noiseless inland solitudes away from main and public roads. A walk with Maxie is always a pleasant, enjoyable experience. Each time I go with him I am enchanted by his delightful sense of wonder and joy. Every bush, every tree, every flower, every curve of the road is something to be explored and to be happy about. Sometimes he runs a long way ahead and then prospects his way back; other times he trails behind lingering and rummaging through some undergrowth pathway. Young children and dogs have that godlike sense of wonder which many of us adults have lost:

> *The angels keep their ancient places*
> *Turn but a stone, and start a wing,*
> *'Tis you, 'tis your estranged faces*
> *That miss the many-splendoured thing.*

We strolled along together away beyond the village, into the countryside, until we found a meandering little by-road, soft and hushed, with only the twittering of the birds and the small sounds of insects in the grass soothing the still calm air. It was the kind of road that goes anywhere and yet goes nowhere, a road that seemed to have no beginning or no ending. Generations must have used it for thousands of years and future generations would surely use it thousands of years hence. We swung along together at one with the rythm of life, listening to the singing birds, and the hum of the bees foraging through the primroses and cowslips that lined the grassy margins. The happy hand of summer tinged every leaf and branch with green. Sometimes the sun came through the foliage, sometimes there was only shadow. God's wonderful sunshine finds its way into the obscure corners of Ireland as well as the arid sands of Teneriffe. We walked along this secret road for nearly an hour until we came to a bend near a little streamlet, and there we met the first human being.

He was a tramp of the old school. He sat by the stream tending a blackened billy-can which he was boiling on a fire of dry twigs. Having eyed Maxie a little uneasily for a moment, he greeted me and asked if I would not care to take my ease and have a 'heat of the tea'. I sat down on a flat stone by the side of the ditch and we began to talk. He was a low-sized man in his late sixties, with a black overgrown beard which only partly covered the healed traces of the cuts and bruises of many a hard-fought brawl in the distant past. Behind this ravaged face, however, one could discern a very deep sense of beauty. He had a merry, sympathetic twinkle in his dark brown eyes which were shaded by the bushiest eyebrows I have ever seen. His hair was wild like a thistle, sparse and unruly, except for one bare spot, the remains of an old wound. His battered hat was upsidedown on the grass and he used it as a hold-all for an assortment of cheese, bread, eggs, tea and other foods. When I told him that I hadn't met a lone travelling man since I was a boy, he agreed that in these times while there were still a good few around, there were not as many as in the old days. 'Long ago, in my father's time, there were hundreds on the road but the Black-and-Tans killed them all. Every time they'd see a travellin' man from their passin' lorries they'd take a shot at him for fun, and if they hit him they'd lave him there to die. I can tell you that kind of conduct thinned out the likes of me a lot. But even if it never happened there wouldn't be as many on the road today. Don't you see, there's too much goin' for nothin' nowadays. A man doesn't even have to get up off his backside to get paid and fed by the government. 'Tis a fool would work. But 'twasn't like that in the ould days. There was no regular work and you couldn't earn as much as you'd jingle on a gravestone, so there was nothin' for it but to take to the road and follow your chances.' He didn't spend all the year travelling, he explained. When the weather was too severe he'd stay in a poorhouse. 'But when the cowld goes out of the wind,' he sighed; 'and the seagulls starts to cry then something inside me starts to cry too and I have to gather my belongings and hit the road.' As he spoke these words, I understood Gerald Gould's feelings:

> *I know not where the white road runs nor what the*
> *blue hills are*
> *But a man can have the sun for a friend, and for his*
> *guide a star;*
> *And there's no end of travelling when once the voice*
> *is heard,*
> *For the river calls and the road calls, and oh! the call*
> *of a bird!*

'Do you find it hard in the poorhouse?' I asked.

'Ah, 'tisn't too bad,' he answered. 'The grub is good enough but the tea does by very light and I likes mine good and strong—and as black as the Earl of Hell's riding boots,' he added with a grin. 'They give you a bed and the run of your teeth and once a week a small bit of tobacco that wouldn't make enough smoke for benediction. Sometimes 'tis hard to sleep at night in a big room with a lot of other ould men, for they do be snorin' and fartin' and talkin' and makin' noise like bluebottles in a butterbox. I can't complain too much about the nuns either, only they're always fussin' and prayin' and I can tell you they're very fond of the soap and water. They'd have you washin' yourself all day. Once a week you'd have to stand in your pelt with a lot of others in one of them wash-houses they call "showers". I don't hould with that. I mean the washin' is all right but why should you have to let every Tom, Dick and Harry see the private parts God gave you? When I asked the nuns for a togs they only laughed at me but faith I got the better of them. I stole the Reverend Mother's bloomers off the line one day and I'm wearin' it ever since in them showers. I wouldn't mind being in me pelt if I had something to show,' he added with a laugh, 'but at my age what I have left is no better than the end tassel on an ould woman's shawl. But smart an' all as the nuns think they are they can be bested. There was an ould fellow from the west years ago and when he came into a poorhouse the first thing he did was to send for a solicitor and give him a fiver to make a will. In the will he left everything he had, over ten thousand pounds, to the nuns in the poorhouse. I can tell you they knew which side their bread was buttered on, and they nursed him and gave special food and extra tobacco and anything he wanted. After five or maybe half-a-dozen years he died and when the nuns went about getting the money they found he hadn't a penny—the will was all a cod. Wasn't he the smart boyo now? Ever since then there's no nun in any poorhouse who would believe the daylights from the likes of me.'

He was a natural conversationalist and storyteller, and was one of those men who, with even a little education, could have been a great novelist or a poet. He talked freely about his youth, manhood and way of life. 'I was born and bred on the side of the road,' he recalled, 'and reared in me bare feet 'till I was fifteen — 'twas then I got me first pair of boots. Me father stole them from a hawker at Cahermee fair. They were a bit small for me and wasn't I the innocent fooleen to go and get a bread-knife to see if I could cut a skelp of skin off me heels to make them fit. By the luck of God me mother caught me in time and whipped the knife off me. Then she rubbed a lot of goose-grease to the boots and left them there for a week to soften out. After that they fitted me like a stockin' and I was so proud that I slept with them on me for a week. Me father and mother slept in a tent of their own and we slept under the axle of the cart with the ends and sides covered with canvas. I never remember bein' hungry, and we always had enough to eat and some of it was the best of grub. Don't you see we had a lurcher dog. Most travelling people had a lurcher dog; that's a cross between a greyhound and a setter. All you have to do is take the dog for a stroll wherever there's pheasants. The setter part of him will scent them out and the greyhound part of him will spring on them before they have time to fly away. So we always had plenty of pheasant to eat and we was never short of a bit of salmon either for me father was a dab hand at tickling fish.'

'Did you never think of taking a steady job?' I asked.

'Ah! the devil on it, I tried a few times but I couldn't stick it,' he answered. 'I always wanted to be on the move. I had a great job one time mindin' a baboon in a circus. All I had to do was feed him, keep his cage clean, and when the circus would move from town to town stay inside in the cage with him in case he got into any trouble. Well things went grand for a spell until the winter came and I can tell you the cowld would cut through you in a cage on the back of an open lorry. Well to keep myself warm I used to bring a half pint of whiskey with me and sup it away to keep the bit of heat in. But the baboon felt the cowld as well, and in order to keep him warm I used to give him a sup too, for we was great friends don't you see. Anyway to make a long story short the two of us was alcoholics before the winter was out. We'd get blind drunk every day on the back of the lorry and then sleep it off till 'twas time for the baboon to go into the ring. Well this day we were travelling over a mountainy road and I was after gettin' a sup of poteen the night before, and we weren't an hour on the road when the two of us was footless. We was so drunk that our brains was in stirabout. I was singin' *Faith of Our Fathers* — I gets very religious when I has a sup in — and the baboon was singin' it with me and tryin' to make the sign of the cross. Anyway after a while I took a bit of a rest and lit a fag and the baboon was so drunk that he demanded one too. I thought I'd better give him a few pulls so I took the fag out of me mouth and put it into his, but me eyes weren't too steady and I put the wrong end into his mouth by mistake. He left a roar out of him that would wake the dead, and he jumped on top of me and took a piece out of the side of me head and ate it. Look, you can see the spot here,' — and he pointed out a scar I had noticed earlier. 'Well I spent eight weeks in hospital and I can give you my word I never want to mate up with a baboon again. That finished me with steady jobs. I'd rather take me chances travellin' the countryside where I could keep myself warm walkin' the roads, or maybe curled up in a snug haybarn 'longside a friendly sheep dog that would keep the bit of heat in you when there's frost in the air.'

I asked him if he ever got married or ever felt the inclination to take a woman. 'Yerra no,' he answered thoughtfully. 'I seen too much trouble and too much fightin' between husbands and wives ever to take a chance on it. You'd want to be real smart to handle a woman. They say you'd want the brains of De Valera and the balls of a Munster Fruslier. But I did think about it once. I was workin' for a fowl-buyer one time pluckin' feathers and he tried to fix me up with a servant girl who was dishin' for his mother, who lived a bit away. Anyhow I said to meself there was no point in lettin' the hare sit too long and I'd better have a look at her first, so early one Sunday morning I walked the eight miles to where she lived and I seen her comin' from last Mass. Well by God you never saw anything like her. She had an arse the size of the Treaty Stone in Limerick and she had a pair of boobs like the buffers on the half-six express from Cork. She had a mouth that stretched from ear to ear and I'd swear me oath if you was givin' her holy communion you could give it to her on a shovel. Be God that was enough for me and I turned on me heel and ran home as fast as the divil ran from the holy water the night of Dan the Gander's wake. That was the nearest I ever came to it. Anyway I'd be no good for a woman. I'd always be wanderin'. When I'd see the top of a hill I wouldn't rest aisy till I saw what was on the other side. I has no time either for any of them quality that does be doin' good and tryin' to get the likes of me to live in a house. All they are doin' is talkin' through their backsides and 'twould be fitter if they stitched them up and minded their own business. I'm happy as I am. Every summer I walk the length and breadth of Ireland. I have a good life and no complaints. Even if I haven't everything in this world, maybe I'd have the upper half of the ladder in the next. God is good.' He began to gather up his utensils as if preparing to move off.

'Have you anywhere to sleep tonight?' I asked, wondering what my two companions would think if I brought him back to the boat. 'Indeed I have,' he said, 'I have regular houses where I calls and gets a nights sleep. They know me well. They lets me sleep in the loft or in the haybarn and gives me the breakfast in the mornin' in return for a couple of hours work — usually to clean out the privy. I don't mind doin' that, because, don't you see I have a touch of them things they calls hadenoids. It would be right tough if I hadn't these friends, and I know because I had to find out the hard way. Some of them well-to-do farmers is so mean that they wouldn't give you the itch even if they had two coats of it; and the meal you'd get from them would be as small as a daisy in an elephant's mouth. But I have me friends, good dacent farmers, and I'm never for the want of a doss for the night.' As I was leaving I slipped a pound into his hand. He looked amazed and taken aback. 'I wasn't expecting or looking for that,' he remarked. 'Keep it anyway,' I answered. 'And maybe some day you'll drink my health?' He stepped over towards me and shook my hand. 'By God I will,' he replied. 'By God I will!' And then as I moved off he called after me jovially; 'Good luck now, and may you be in heaven two hours before the divil finds out you're dead.'

As I lazily sauntered back to Dromineer, surrounded by all the enchanting wildings of a mysterious nature, I fell to thinking how lucky I was to be cruising the Shannon and honoured by such exceptional company as the tramp I had just left. He was a gentleman of nature, a man at one with the beauty of the world, the mystery of loneliness, the beating heart of life. He ate close to the earth and watched the stars as he slept at night. He rambled the roads of Ireland the slave of no man. He had no appointments diary, no telephone, no expense account, and his soul was not handcuffed to the cruel hands of any clock. He was a realist, raw and earthy. He did not pretend to be other than what he was, an ordinary tramp. He was poor in the things that money can buy, but extremely rich in those things money

43

cannot buy. He could talk on many subjects with a wisdom that had a thousand years tradition behind it. His eyes looked into the face of life and saw the face of God. To have met him and conversed with him was like listening to the song of a lark in the clear air or the scent of a field of new-mown hay in summer.

The evening was slowly dreaming it's way into twilight when I got back on board. My two companions had an excellent dinner cooked but they were deeply disappointed with their fishing trip. Not only did they catch no fish, but they did not even see one. Lough Derg, which was once teeming with fish of every kind, is now almost as barren as the Dead Sea. It is being polluted indiscriminately. Its great days were now over and will never return. After dinner we rambled up the village and into the bar of the 'Sail Inn' where Juliana Roberts made us heartily welcome, and as so often happens, it was not long before we got ourselves involved with a group of Frenchmen who were also cruising. It looked as if it were going to be a right merry, lively night, but because I was tired after the long walk and I was making valiant efforts to get my weight down, I left after two drinks, returned on board and went to bed.

Next morning Maxie woke me rubbing his nose against my cheek, something he does regularly and with positive effect. I got up, and after a quick wash and shave, brought him ashore for his usual run. This first run in the morning is a very happy one for him. He jumps and frolics and rolls over as if to bid welcome to the new day. Once again it was another lovely summer's morning. Luck had so far favoured us; the lake can be really nasty and repellant in bad conditions, but there was no sign of the weather breaking. There was as yet very little wind. In the distance the slow-moving clouds wove themselves fold upon fold along the mountain tops. The young sun was dancing on the waters of the lake and I knew that we had another magnificent day before us. We planned to cruise up to Terryglass, and finally north to Portumna, where we intended to stay the night.

But there was no hurry upon us. When God was making time he made enough of it, as they say in Tipperary, so after breakfast which we enjoyed on deck, we went for a stroll along the shores of the lake to the next little bay, called Launagower. Twenty years ago Launagower was a miniature Garden of Eden; a chequer-board of heath and glebe, hill and knoll, purple heather, and golden whin interwined to make an undergrowth where the foxes, hares and rabbits made their hidden earthy homes. A woodland of oak, elm, sycamore and ash edged the shore of the lake. Here the squirrels jumped and gambolled from tree to tree and hundreds of singing birds built their cosy nests and sang out the secrets of their hearts to every passer-by. Along the labyrinthine pathways wild flowers, buttercups and ferns gladdened the heart of every dawdling wayfarer. And through it all ran a little playful steam on a floor of glistening pebbles. There young boys and girls spent the carefree summer days climbing trees, chasing rabbits, fishing with nets and jam-jars in the little stream, at one with nature and in harmony with the magnificent surroundings. But a killing blight has crept over Launagower and destroyed the beauty and adventure of this by-gone paradise. Bulldozers have moved in and flattened the knolls and hillocks, ripped by the roots the whins, the heather and the wild flowers, and strangled this delightful paradise of nature into a car park, with round-abouts and floats, contraptions which belong to the concrete of the city and not to the countryside. Today the children play on these man-made frameworks, and know nothing of the natural playground which once thrilled their fathers. Pollution of all kinds has killed the hares, the rabbits and the birds. The remaining woodland is now impregnated with the silence of death. As we strolled along, saddened and depressed by what we saw, we turned over some of the larger stones at the water's edge. Normally we should see shrimps, water-beetles and other shore life scampering away; but there was nothing to be seen. The life on the lake's edge was dead too. And so we left this monument to an indifferent generation, our generation unwittingly destroying the beauty of the Irish countryside.

Out once more on the lake we set our course for Terry-glass. The water was calm. The distant hills were drenched in sunlight and the clouds of the early morning had dissolved into a blue sky. As we drew close to the black buoy off Urra Point I could see St David's house in all its splendour. In the last century St David's was the home of one of Ireland's greatest eccentrics and practical jokers. His name was Traherne Holmes, a man of the last century, whose fame travelled much farther than his native Tipperary. It is said that he had some dispute with the Dromineer Yacht Club, as a result of which it was made quite clear to him that he was no longer welcome in that club. The story is told that when Dromineer were holding a rather exclusive garden fete on the lawn near the lake in aid of the Killaloe cathedral fund, Traherne swam across in the nude from St David's with only a bowler hat on his head. When he reached the shore he covered his private parts with the hat and boldly walked up among the distinguished guests to the open-air bar, filled himself a tumbler of champagne, drank it and walked quickly back to the lake, still barely covered by the hat. The bishop, the dean, the canons, the colonels and their ladies could hardly speak with fury, but as he was nearing the shore three young girls burst out laughing at him. Holmes took them to task: 'How dare you laugh at me!' he exclaimed angrily, 'have you no manners?' 'Your own manners are nothing to write home about,' was the smart reply. 'Don't you know you should always raise your hat before your address ladies!' Whereupon Holmes being the perfect gentleman, hid behind a bush that covered his lower parts, raised his hat smartly and bowed gallantly. Etiquette was satisfied. He was in the habit of riding around the countryside on a magnifient horse and occasionally he got drunk and slept in the ditch. When that happened some friendly neighbour usually found him and brought him home. One night, according to the story, he was in a drunken sleep in a ditch near Nenagh, when two friends, a little more sober than himself, picked him up in their pony-and-trap, intending to bring him home. But as they were passing the graveyard they decided to play a practical joke on him for a change. Traherne was still asleep when his two friends carried him in, put him down into an open grave that was dug for a funeral the following day, and left him there. Holmes dined out on this incident for years afterwards, and he usually ended his discourse by describing the shock he got when he woke up the next morning. 'I stood up in the grave, gentlemen,' he would say. 'I was barely tall enough to look out and when I saw all the crosses, monuments and tombstones around me I thought it was the Last Day and I was the first up!'

St David's, the home of this delightful character, faded from our sight as we passed the Carrikeen Islands and out into the main stream of the lake. We did not feel the time going until we reached the dangerous Benjamin Rocks and then on to our next buoy at Goat Island. Ahead of us on the Galway shore we could see Rossmore pier but we avoided the temptation to go in. This is a delightful little pier at the mouth of the meandering Woodford River, set in the most romantic, secluded loneliness, and suitable only for poets, lovers and honeymoon couples. But it was not always so. In the dim and distant past, long long before you or I were born, the merchants of Galway complained bitterly that they were being constantly robbed of their merchandise in this very harbour by outlaws whom they claimed were 'the bastard sons of the lord bishop of Killaloe!' But the outlaws are no more, and bishops are better behaved, and today Rossmore is a shaded haven of beauty and peace. We passed Kilgarvan harbour by, because from past experience I do not find this anchorage so attractive. The berthing is small, it is awkward and difficult to turn if there are many other boats around. A new harbour was recently built but it is unsuitable for cruisers, because it is so shallow and, because of the ever-present danger of the ESB dropping the level of the lake without notice or warning which could leave one high and dry for days or even weeks.

Slowly the golden hours passed by until we picked out the Kylnoe Rocks, then Gortmore Point and finally Terryglass harbour where we tied up alongside another boat at the crowded jetty. Here we had a late but welcome lunch and then set out to visit the little village and the monastic settlement founded there in the sixth century. A pleasant walk along a shady country road brought us into Terryglass itself. This unpretentious hamlet was once the site of one of the most celebrated centres of learning in Ireland. It was the final resting place of Flann, one of the greatest of Irish poets, who was known as the Devil's Son, and local tradition holds that he returned home to his reputed father when he died. We went into the old graveyard where the great monastery once flourished but little now remains. It also seems as if there is little or nothing left of Terryglass Castle, which belonged to the O'Kennedys. When the last of that clan was thrown from the battlements, they say Brian Boru's banshee came up from Killaloe and mourned and wailed for nine days and nine nights. We asked a local if he could direct us to the castle but he apologetically explained that he was only a few years living in the area and he didn't remember any castle being built. We had a drink or two in the village and rambled back at our ease to the jetty. On our way we fell to discussing Flann, the roguish poet of Terryglass, poetry, poets and literature, and it occurred to us that a powerful Irish novel could be written using the story of Judkin Fitzgerald as its inspiration. Fitzgerald was one of the most vicious sadists in the whole bloody history of Ireland. He was a renegade Irishman who went over to the service of the British and held the office of Sheriff for north Tipperary. After the 1798 rebellion he rampaged all around this peaceful countryside, which was not really involved in any kind of hostilities, calling on almost every house, flogging old men, women and children and then forcing them on their knees to pray for King George. He had a special gallows erected in front of his stately house and anyone who showed the slightest spark of independence, or answered him back, he hung them promptly. In this way many hundreds of innocent Tipperary men and women went to their deaths. Then one day, according to local tradition, his nine year old son was proudly showing some visiting English schoolboys how his father hung Irishmen, and while demonstrating how the gallows worked the noose suddenly closed on the boy's neck and he was strangled to death. After the child's funeral the distracted Fitzgerald hung himself on the same scaffold. Here are all the stark, grim elements of the great Russian tragedies on our own doorstep. The novel could be called, simply, *The Gallows*. It is a theme, we felt, well worthy of the pen of our best novelists, or indeed of our greatest dramatist, John B. Keane.

From Terryglass to Portumna, where we would spend the night, is only a short distance of four miles, and as we left we could see the steeple of Portumna church like a finger admonishing all doers of wrong, and warning us to behave ourselves when we went ashore. We passed through the four buoys of Derry Point and finally entered the lordly Shannon River:

> *River of Chieftains whose baronial halls*
> *Like veteran wardens watch each wave-worn steep,*
> *Portumna's towers, Bunratty's royal walls,*
> *Carrick's stern rock, the Geraldine's grey keep*
> *River of dark mementoes! must I close*
> *My lips with Limerick's wrong, with Aughrim's woes!*

We arrived just in time to get through the opening bridge and into the Connaught harbour where, by the kindness of *Emerald Star Line*, we found a snug berth for the night.

After dinner we strolled along a pleasant path, past tastefully decorated houses and gardens, into the town of Portumna itself. At the post office we wrote our greeting cards, made telephone calls and let our relatives know we were still alive and well. We rambled for nearly an hour through the beautiful woodland park where once no Irishman dared set foot, but where now the people of Portumna can walk in peace and enjoy the whispering sounds of evening and the radiant beauty of the long summer days. On our way back we visited the ruins of Portumna Castle, in the last century the home of Lord Clanrickarde, who was one of the most inhuman landlords in the whole history of that hated breed of oppressors. I had heard a lot about this Clanrickarde, whose income, all from rack rents, was greater than that of the King of England himself, but I could find very little published material on his activities. It is said that most journalists were afraid to write the truth about him for fear of a devastating revenge. One English writer who said, 'the day will come when Clanrickarde will meet his Waterloo' was sentenced to a long term of imprisonment on a trumped-up charge. I was, therefore, very glad when, later in the evening in a pleasant pub, I met an intelligent local who remembered hearing the whole Clanrickarde saga from his grandfather, one of the thousands evicted by this gallant lord.

'Clanrickarde wasn't an exception,' he explained. 'Most of the landlords were cruel and inhuman. If only they were as well bred as they were fed they might be gentlemen, but the majority were descended from the very scum of Elizabeth's armies and indeed if their pedigrees had to be recorded in a stud-book that book would surely be banned. The worst period here around Portumna was the last quarter of the nineteenth century. Clanrickarde inherited 52,000 acres of land producing a rent of £25,000 per annum – equivalent to £500,000 in today's money. He lived in bloated luxury in London and never visited the estate since he inherited it in 1873, or never spent a penny on improvements. The year 1879 was a bad year of famine and crop failure in Ireland and the wolfish eye of hunger swept through the land. A few decent landlords in the country waived all rents that year, but not so Clanrickarde. He evicted thousands of men, women and children and left them starving to death in the fields around Portumna, and worse still the London government provided his agent with 150 armed British troops to carry out these ejectments. In an effort to teach him a lesson a distant kinsman of my own, and a few other starving peasants shot dead his agent, Blake, but this did not deter him. Of course the mistake they made was that they did not cross to London and shoot Clanrickarde himself. Eviction followed eviction. The painful death agonies of starving women and children were to be heard and seen daily on the roadsides and even on the streets of Portumna itself. But those brave people believed that it was better to die than yield to a tyrant and, in the end, at a terrible cost in lives and suffering, they defeated Clanrickarde. Under Parnell they used the 'boycott weapon' and Clanrickarde failed to get any grabber to rent his lands. Most of those lands are now owned by the descendants of the people he evicted and Clanrickarde is gone with not even a headstone to mark his overgrown and neglected grave.' He paused for a few moments, re-lit his pipe, and continued. 'But perhaps the saddest thing of all, is, that if you look around Portumna for a memorial to those brave thousands who starved to death and made the Ireland of today possible, you will not find any. But what will you find? Clanrickarde's Castle, which should have been razed to the ground, is being restored to all it's full splendour. The Irish government is providing hundreds of thousands of pounds out of your pocket and mine, to perpetuate the memory of this tyrant at a time when scores of national monuments all over the country are being refused badly needed funds. An old teacher of mine used to say that slavery degrades men to the extent of making them love it, and it seems as if we surely love it. Is it any wonder that we are thought of throughout Europe as a nation of toadies?' He slowly finished his drink and called for another round. 'Did you know that Clanrickarde was once a respected Irish name and that before they turned their coats a Clanrickarde died fighting for the Irish at Aughrim? Davis remembered him:

Oft when in O'Connor's van
To triumph dashed each Connaught clan
And fleet as deer the Normans ran

51

Through Curlew's pass and Ardrahan
And later days saw deeds as brave
And glory guards Clanrickarde's grave
Sing oh! they died their land to save
'Neath Aughrim slopes and Shannon's wave.

The last drinks arrived as it was near closing time. I asked him about present-day Portumna. 'Portumna is a cheerful self-respecting town of very decent people,' he replied with a touch of pride in his voice. 'But like many another Irish town violence has caught up with it. Some years ago it was particularly noted for its picturesque and tasteful appearance when every street and house displayed many window boxes of multi-coloured flowers. But the young vandals, the young Bugsie Malones, put an end to that. Our streets are still clean and tidy but somewhat spartan. We have hardly any people who prefer the dole to work. The strike disease has not yet hit us and I do not think it will. We have pleasant parks and woodlands and of course the lovely Shannon on our doorstep. All in all, compared to many other towns we have every reason to be contented. God made enough for the needy,' he added with a smile, 'but not for the greedy.' The owner of the pub was now courteously nudging his talkative customers homewards, so I bade goodbye to my comrade of the evening and, together with Maxie and my two companions, made my way back through the still summer night to the jetty and to a welcome sleep.

3

After a late and somewhat lazy breakfast next morning my companions went into Portumna to buy the papers and to replenish other supplies needed for the day's journey. I took Maxie into the punt and went rowing around the river, with no particular purpose in mind other than the vague general pleasure of idling close to the water. I paddled along by the edge of the tall reeds that swayed in the morning sunlight, now towering above me for all the world like the spears of an invading army. Maxie thought, because there were reeds growing, that it was dry land and impulsively jumped after a moor-hen only to find himself in several feet of choked water struggling to keep afloat. I got him back on board again and crossed the river to where the old Munster harbour was in the long ago days of the canal men and their barges. It is now overgrown, desolate and sad, a decaying memory of a world that is past and gone. I rowed idly along the bank in the warm freshness of the summer morning, the sunlight sparkling on the wet oars, a gentle breeze barely caressing the surface of the water, until I came upon what I was to see quite often on the Shannon, a visiting fisherman, with his huge coloured umbrella, boxes of bait and many rods. I pulled alongside and we started chatting. The fishing was fairly good, he said. The catch was mostly bream, rudd and perch. But indeed it was not so much the fishing, as the peace and quiet, that attracted him. He returned most of the fish to the river, he told me, and only kept one or two for his supper. But to be able to sit on the bank, away from the noise of a city, in God's clean air was, he said, the best holiday he could imagine. He kindly invited me to a cup of coffee from his flask but I explained that I had just had my breakfast. We chatted and talked about a whole lot of things. He lived in a big English city and was spending two weeks of perfect laziness in the Portumna area, he said. He usually spent a spell on the banks of the Shannon each year, though not always in the same place. As I often do when I strike up an acquaintance with a stranger, I was trying to figure out what he did for a living and, after some speculation, I came to the conclusion that, because of his precise manner, he was an executive of some sort. Indeed I was far off the mark. He later revealed that he was an undertaker's assistant and specialised in the washing and laying out of corpses, and in various other

53

matters pertaining to the preparation of man for his journey to the next world. He was informative rather than talkative, and it took only a little diplomatic questioning to start him off on his life story.

'A lot of people think,' he explained, 'that laying out corpses is child's play but I can tell you it is highly skilled handiwork. In a way it is like one of those beauty parlours except that I'm doing them up for the last time for a fairly long journey and I have to make them look as if they were enjoying every minute of it.' He was not sparing with the grim details. 'First of all you must give them a good scrubbing and block up all the openings in the lower part of the body. Champagne corks are best for this because they won't pop out too easily. In the case of a man, as well as giving him a good shave, you have to tie up his lower machinery with twine. You see you have to be very careful with such matters just in case there would be an sudden motion in these parts during the wake or funeral. I remember a case where the undertaker did a bad job and the corpse broke wind and let off a lot of vulgar noises during the High Mass. To make matters worse everyone thought that the hullabaloo came from the canon who was getting on in years and inclined to fall asleep and forget himself during services. You have to make their faces look a lot younger than they are. You can do this by putting a little plaster-of-paris inside their jaws, that will take every wrinkle away. The relatives appreciate it very much for they like to be able to say: "Doesn't he look very happy? He's surely with God and his angels." Last year I did a job on a man who died suddenly on vacation in a seaside resort and I laid him out so satisfactorily — I gave him a bit of a tan, don't you see — that everyone who saw him in the coffin remarked on how well he looked after his holidays. You have to try to please the relations at all costs because they're inclined to be a bit free with the money, and you could come well out of it yourself. I suppose it is how having blackguarded the man during his life that they want to make up for it when he's dead.' We discoursed a bit

54

further on this sombre subject and when I asked him what was the proudest moment in his career he had no trouble in recollecting it. It came when he was asked to lay out a bishop.

'I'm not ashamed to admit I was very proud of that job,' he said. 'And I got all my work-mates and friends in the trade to come and view him. I made absolutely sure there would be no vulgar noises for I used the best putty with a hardener. I dressed him up in his mitre, white gloves and all his red pontificals, and, if I may say so without disrespect, he looked the living image of a fresh lobster on the sideboard of a first class hotel. I was so proud I couldn't keep me eyes off him while he was lying in state, and I used to spend the evenings in the church just sitting there watching the crowds admiring my handiwork.' I asked him how he got into this particular business and he explained that he grew up with it from childhood. 'We lived on a small scab of land in Ireland and we were nearly twenty miles from the nearest doctor or nurse. My mother was what you would call a handy-woman; that is, she cured measles, whooping cough, piles, thrush and the itch. She also washed all the corpses and laid them out in the coffin. She learned it all from her mother and her mother's mother; it was handed down for generations in our family. She also delivered babies into the world. I can tell you she knew a lot of secrets, and I often heard her saying that there was far more fathers in the parish than husbands. When we were young he used to give her a hand with the corpses. I remember when I was about twelve years of age we were washing an old farmer with a long white beard, like that fellow in the papers, the Ayatolla. He was dead a day or two before he was found so that in order to keep his mouth shut we had to put a sod of turf under his chin — it was hidden by the beard, don't you see. So as to keep his feet up straight we had to tie his two big toes together with binder twine. Any way my sister, who was then about seventeen years, was helping my mother. We were washing him in a room off the kitchen and they sent me out to the pump in the back yard to get another bucket of water. I filled the bucket and carried it in but it was so heavy I had to rest it for a minute in the middle of the kitchen floor. Then I heard my sister saying to my mother inside in the room: "Mammy, I always thought there was a bone in that thing." No sooner had she the words out of her mouth when my mother levelled her with a belt in the jaw, and then got a whip that was near the dresser and started to flake her with it until the poor girl ran out of the house roaring crying and away home with her as fast as her legs could carry her. It seemed an innocent enough remark and at first I didn't really understand why my mother was so cross, until I heard her shouting after my sister: "How do you know it should be stiff, you little tramp?" 'Twas then I understood my mother's worry. I can tell you she was a strict woman and she reared us all in the fear and love of God, which is more than can be said for some of the mothers nowadays. So you see I grew up with dead people you might say, and I found it the most natural thing in the world to turn them to account. I'm an expert at my job and right proud of my work. A side of it where you have to have great skill is putting corpses together after an accident, and, if I may say so, I can dress them up without a mark in a way you'd think they were going to a wedding. I only made one real mistake in my whole life and that was a long time ago when four people were killed in a car crash, and I got the job of putting them together. I was young then and I took a few drinks to give me courage. Unfortunately, I put a man's head on a woman's body and the relatives couldn't understand how he grew two breasts since he died. I nearly got sacked for that one, but good enough, my boss consoled the people by telling them that they were only swellings that would be gone in a week. That seemed to satisfy them. That wasn't the only time I got into trouble. Once for leaving a man's horn-rimmed glasses on him when I was closing the lid of the coffin, and another time when I was driving a horse-drawn hearse, dressed in top-hat and white sash, I winked at a good-looking girl I saw on the street and she complained me to the boss. He was furious that I should do this when heading a funeral, and I had to get an M.P. and two councillors to get me out of that bit of trouble. All the same I wouldn't change my job for anything and I'm doing my best to put my children into the business. I have one son learning the trade with myself, and another son, who's not very bright, doing well selling Japanese coffins.'

At this very moment his cork began to bob violently. He tightened his line and it was clear that he had hooked a a good fish. He played him steadily and carefully for a few minutes and then I helped him with the net. It was a fine two-and-a-half or three pound bream. 'I have my dinner now,' he exclaimed with delight. I thought this an opportune moment to leave him and as I said goodbye and pushed off in the punt he laughingly called after me: 'You brought me luck! You brought me luck! When it happens to you, tell your relations to contact me. I'll come over and do a right good job on you. I'll deck you up in a way that when you arrive at the gates of heaven 'tis how St Peter will think you're some big star from Hollywood and he'll give you a chair to sit down and he'll ask you for your autograph!'

Coming up towards midday we sailed out of Connaught harbour and into the broad magnificence of the Shannon, leaving the woods, the hills and the elegant houses around Portumna behind us as we moved into the great central plain of Ireland. All along here the land is very flat, with houses built rather far back as a protection against the sometimes devastating winter floods. But these same floods give the land a luxurious richness, and colour its many shades of green with contrasting patches of dreamy buttercup and wild iris which sometimes seem to set the gently sloping fields on flame. The day itself was throbbing with life. The swallows swooped and dived towards the water in search of flies; scattered flocks of wild ducks chattered to themselves high up in the clear blue sky; brown and white speckled calfs gambolled and romped in the fields near the water's edge. Maxie moved restlessly up and down the deck as if he wanted to jump ashore and join in the fun. We passed Portland Island where in the eighteenth century a young Irish chieftain named O'Connell hid with the only daughter of Lord Clanrickarde after they had eloped. But she was accidentally drowned while trying to reach the eastern bank on a small raft. The old bargemen will tell you that her ghost is still wandering around the island, and a local ballad commemorates the event:

> *Though time has since flown fast away*
> *The Shannon rolls as ever*
> *And oft upon a moonlit bay*
> *That hems the noble river*
> *The midnight wanderer has espied*
> *A steed while o'er the water*
> *A tiny bark is seen to glide*
> *With Clanrickarde's only daughter.*

Further on we passed Ballymacegan Island where the great O'Sullivan Bere made his crossing of the Shannon in his famous retreat from Glengarriff to Leitrim. Lord Mountjoy, with a large English army, was systematically slaughtering the population of West Cork with incredible brutality, and this made O'Sullivan decide to move his entire clan to O'Rourke territory in the north where he would be safer. In the depth of a terrible winter he left Glengarriff with six hundred women and children and four hundred troops and a month later when they arrived in Leitrim there were only thirty-five souls left. Hunger, exposure and the attacks of English patrols and the treachery of some Irish tribes had reduced them to this number. When they arrived on the east bank of the Shannon, north of Portumna, they found that all ferries and boats had been withdrawn by English collaborators. They camped just opposite the island we were now passing, and constructed a number of crude rafts to make the crossing. One of the arch-quislings of the time, Donnacha Mac Egan from nearby Redwood Castle, waited until most of the soldiers had crossed and then mercilessly attacked the women and children. But O'Sullivan had left a patrol of seasoned troops behind to protect the east bank. This patrol fell upon Mac Egan, killed himself and his entire raiding party, and saved the helpless civilians. People still point out a spot on the river called Poll na gCapall where hunger forced them to eat the flesh of Mac Egan's dead horses and use the skins to construct rafts. The incident is still remembered in a local ballad:

> *Mac Egan's wrath there barred our path*
> *But we gave him warning early*
> *To clear our way or his band we'd slay*
> *And we kept our promise fairly*
> *Each killed a steed in that hour of need*
> *After false Mac Egan slaughter*
> *Curraghs unstaid of their skins we made*
> *And crossed the Shannon's water.*

A short distance beyond Ballymacegan Island the blue and white of the great Meelick Lock came into view. This is the largest lock on the cruising part of the Shannon, and it was built in 1840 by a nameless army of Irish slaves many of whom had to walk barefooted ten or fifteen miles to work from six o'clock in the morning to six o'clock in the evening for the princely sum of threepence per day. When it was all over, a cynical local once told me, and they faced the famine with nothing, they had the consolation of knowing that it was called after Queen Victoria as we have the joy of knowing that it still bears her name. A certain amount of caution is necessary when approaching the little quay below the lock where one waits until it opens. Just ahead of the last red perch there seems to be a mud-bank reaching from centre way across to the east bank. Once or twice I have gone aground here and nearly choked the engine water-intake. So we thought it best to keep close to the western shore and as soon as we came level with the quay we cut straight across and moored astern of another cruiser flying the German flag. The lock-keepers had just gone for their lunch so we had to wait an hour or thereabouts until they returned. After a quick snack my two companions went fishing in the punt up the little Brosna river, while Maxie and myself went rambling around the fields and pathways that reach down to the old canal and the ruins of an early lock of the eighteenth century.

It is the little unplanned interludes like this I find so charming about cruising on the Shannon. You quickly come to terms with the inevitable fact that hurry and bustle will get you nowhere, and as you do, all tension and anxiety seem to vanish as an untroubled and mysterious peace casts a spell over your soul. Meelick, almost inaccessible by road, is one of the Shannon's secret places; a place where time stands still and where a weary human spirit can soar above a world of blighted hopes. Having strolled along overgrown pathways for nearly half-an-hour I found a pleasant resting place under a wild hawthorn bush just beginning to drop its blossoms one by one. Maxie lay at my feet, surrounded by a carpet of golden buttercups, still panting after his forays and feats in the world beneath the bushes and trees. In the distance I could hear the soft soothing sound of the murmuring water falling over the salmon weir, like the sound of music lost somewhere in space and contrasting strangely with the little whispering noises that came from the grass and the buzzing of the insects like telegraph wires in a summer's breeze. Everywhere around me birds were singing joyously; blackbird, thrush, goldfinch, starling and many others — Meelick was one of the few places on the Shannon where I heard such a melody of wild song. The whole atmosphere was permeated with the sad loveliness of life. Overhead, a lark, suspended high in the sky dropped golden chords of exquisite music on to the rolling meadows. I envied that lark who had something we humans hadn't, two worlds to live in — the blue sky and the rich earth, and then the words of that most beautiful of Irish songs *The Lark in the Clear Air* tumbled through my head:

60

Dear thoughts are in my mind
And my soul soars enchanted
As I hear the sweet lark sing
In the clear air of the day
For a tender beaming smile
To my hope has been granted
And tomorrow she shall hear
All my fond heart would say.

'The world is a study that did not quite come off,' moaned Van Gogh. I do not agree. We live in a marvellous world but many of us seem to be in too much of a hurry ever to become aware of it. Very often, however, in the quiet moments of a holiday, we get a tiny glimpse of what we are missing, and the beauty all around us stirs up strange vague feelings that are very hard to define, but which give us the sense of a deep incompleteness in our lives. Yet I think if we just pause awhile and not be frightened by this feeling and listen carefully we will hear, not only the music from outside, but an inner music of the soul which harmonises with it, and it will then seem that there is no real division between ourselves and the beauty of the universe. The infinite cannot be divided against itself. Even though man is an insignificant speck he is still part of a God's dream which has no end. 'In a rest which is meditative and attentive,' said Amiel, 'the wrinkles of the soul are smoothed away, and the soul itself spreads, unfolds and springs afresh, and like the trodden grass of the roadside, or the bruised leaf of a plant, repairs its injuries, becomes new, spontaneous, true and original.' There is always a little left from what floats in the wake of our dreams.

Having passed through the lock we continued on up river. Meelick was an important crossing down the centuries. As early as the thirteenth century a de Burgo built a castle there which he used as a base to rob and plunder the surrounding countryside, and at one point he was so powerful that he imprisoned Feilim, King of Connaught, in his dungeons at Meelick. De Burgo became such a nuisance that the

Norman king gave him large tracts of lands further north in Galway, and he abandoned his Shannon fortress and became a respectable member of the aristocracy. This path to respectibility is age-old and survived into modern Irish politics. As we passed Incherky Island the overgrowth blotted out the ruins of the Martello Tower erected in the early 1800s when Napoleon struck terror into the occupying forces in Ireland. There are still to be seen the remains of the iron bolts used for the guns. The word Incherky when translated means 'island of love', and I was most curious as to why and how this particular island got its name. Was it one of those islands where superstition held that lovers never lost their potency and could keep going until sleep overcame them? Or was it simply a secluded place where the young Irish of two thousand years ago besported themselves without the risk of being caught by their parents? On a previous visit I was speculating on this possibility with a young German honeymoon couple whose boat was tied up alongside me at the quay opposite. Later, when I had left for Banagher, I could see behind me the young couple rowing hell-for-leather in the direction of the island. On that occasion I asked a fisherman if he could give me any clue as to how the island got its name. He was a shrewd countryman who, presumably felt it would be bad for tourism if he did not provide an answer. 'I heard the story long ago,' he said very slowly obviously needing time to compose a good tale. ''Tis said that an Irish prince was having a tally with a servant girl that was a lot younger than himself, and they got stuck. They had to stay that way for a whole day until the lord abbot of Clonfert came to the island and threw a firkin of holy water over them. I don't know how true the story is but that's how I heard it from me grandfather.' So long as Ireland has imaginative story-tellers like that we need never fear for our tourist industry. Anyway lets hope the two young Germans did not run into any embarrassing difficulties.

We sailed to the west of Mucknish Island and then into the narrow channel east of the beautiful Inishee, and in a very short time we passed under the navigation arch of the magnificent Banagher bridge, and tied up at the *Silver Line Cruisers* jetty, the homeport of our boat. This little town is one of the most delightful and friendly on the whole Shannon. The first thing that strikes you about Banagher is the sense of good taste with which the old has been made to blend with the new. It is still an old world town but it has almost every facility and service one could reasonably require. The shops are amongst the best stocked on the entire Shannon, not only with run-of-the-mill supermarket goods, but also fine wines, delicatessen foods and crisp, fresh vegetables. The shopkeepers themselves are most helpful, and if you happen to mention you are on a boat all your purchases will be delivered for no extra charge. A visit to the beautiful Crannog pottery just at the entrance to the marina is a most rewarding experience. Here you can find everything worthwhile in arts and crafts, all Irish made and all reflecting in one way or another the traditions of the people. I have visited it many times and I have never been able to drag myself away without making a few purchases, every one of which has given me intense satisfaction. Banagher is a town that has a great historical past. It was here that General Patrick Sarsfield crossed the Shannon on his circuitous route back to Limerick having blown up King William's munition train on its way to demolish the walls of the city. In order to evade the enraged English, who were pursuing him, Sarsfield came as far as Banagher, crossed the Shannon and returned by night to Limerick. It is said that in order to mislead his pursuers he had the shoes put on his horses back to front so that they were bewildered and confused and failed to track him down.

Shortly after Christmas in 1814 the people of Banagher woke up one morning to find the following notice posted up in various parts of the town:

We the parishioners of Lusmagh, give notice to the town of Banagher that we will go in on Thursday next and give them battle. Captain Armstrong says that he will bring his yeomen on us but we defy his best and all the army in the county. We are able to disarm them and take the town ourselves. Richard Woods had a great deal of talk the last day but himself and Boyle and Ramsey and a lot more will rue the hour that we go in.

Captain Stout.

This was a formal notice that a faction fight was about to take place between two parishes whose bitter enmity for each other went back hundreds of years, and is supposed to have started when the Maddens of Banagher killed a Lusmagh chief, Feilim Mac Coghlan, when he was coming out from Mass in Banagher. But the whole thing was a bit of a fiasco. Before the fight could get under way a troop of soldiers arrived and fired on the Lusmagh men, killing four or five, and wounding twelve or fourteen. The rest turned and fled. An old man who died ten years ago at the age of ninety-seven, told me that his great-grandfather fought with the Lusmagh men and often told the story to his great-grandchildren. 'We could have sacked Banagher and levelled it to the ground,' he said. 'But when the soldiers arrived what could we do? We only had sticks and stones against bullets. Our two leaders were shot dead with a lot of others, so there was nothing for it but to gather ourselves home as fast as we could. We never attacked Banagher again for fear of the soldiers.' Thus ended ignominiously what might have been one of the great faction fights of Irish history.

At the eastern end of the town there is a beautiful celtic cross commemorating the execution of two young local men, Barnes and MacCormack, in Birmingham in 1940. The general belief is that this was simply the judicial murder of two innocent people in an act of government revenge. The story began in August 1939 when a young IRA man cycled across Coventry with a prefused bomb in the carrier basket of his bicycle. It was his intention to place it at a power installation where it would have caused considerable damage but would not have killed anyone. It was timed to go off at 2.30 p.m. but the young man had obviously not allowed for heavy traffic and contrary traffic lights. At 2.29 he was not near his destination and as the seconds ticked away he panicked, jumped off and left his bicycle against a wall and ran. The bomb went off, blew up a shop and killed five people. The police raided most Irish homes in Coventry and arrested two IRA members, Peter Barnes and James MacCormack. They never found the man who dropped the bicycle and bomb. Although they had no evidence that either of the two were involved in the killings they were charged with murder and, in a verdict that shocked all right thinking people, even in England, were found guilty and sentenced to death for a murder they did not commit. They made a tremendous impression on the world press by their dignified bearing as they protested their innocence. An intense feeling of sympathy swept over the two countries and thousands of English people, shocked by what they saw to be a miscarriage of British justice, attended protest meetings, but all to no avail; the two young men were hanged. The next day all Ireland went into national mourning. Flags flew at half mast. Places of public entertainment closed. Religious services were held in various churches and a wave of bitterness and hatred against the British government swept the country. Years later the people of Banagher erected this beautiful memorial in memory of two of their most famous sons.

By a strange coincidence another son of Banagher was judicially murdered in 1867. He was Michael Larkin of Lusmagh, one of the famous Manchester Martyrs. Together with William Allen and Michael O'Brien he was executed for the shooting of a police sergeant. None of the three were involved in this crime, but scapegoats had to be found, as in the case of Barnes and MacCormack, and all three were executed. So blatant was the perjury and bias at their trial that thirty newspaper reporters of different nationalities who attended the court petitioned the Home Secretary to the effect that these men were innocent. Having examined the matter the Home Secretary agreed — but it was too late. The executions had taken place. It was this terrible incident that inspired the famous song *God Save Ireland:*

> *High upon the gallows tree*
> *Swung the noble-hearted three,*
> *By the vengeful tyrant striken in their bloom;*
> *But they met him, face to face*
> *With the courage of their race*
> *And they went with souls undaunted to their doom.*
> *God save Ireland, said the heroes*
> *God save Ireland, said they all;*
> *Whether on the scaffold high*
> *Or on battle-field we die*
> *Oh, what matter when for Ireland dear we fall?*

Anthony Trollope, the English novelist, was stationed quite a while in Banagher. He established the rural postal service in Ireland and was reputed to be the inventor of the pillar-box. He made a great deal of money on his novels which were described by one critic as 'like a leg of mutton, substantial but coarse'. Trollope was a hard worker. He wrote 3,000 words every day whether he felt like it or not, and maintained to be a great writer all a man needed was pen and paper and a tin of strong glue to keep his behind stuck to the chair!

Early in the afternoon we managed to get a car and we set out for the beautiful and historic Clonfert Cathedral. It is but a short distance from Banagher over quiet country roads, almost lanes, that give forth a sense of peace appropriate to the precincts of a great monastery. Clonfert is a lonely place today, so lonely that they say that the foxes bid 'good-day' to the dogs. But is was once a great university with more than 3,000 students. It was founded by St Brendan, the great navigator who discovered America, and after a lifetime at sea he turned his thoughts towards the world of learning, and here, at the age of 93, far from the sound of the ocean, he died, having founded one of the greatest of European universities. It was he who said when he was a young monk: 'Lord reform the world, beginning with me.' But Clonfert had its turbulent days. Phelim, a king of Cashel in the ninth century, who was nothing more than a professional robber, plundered Clonfert and made himself abbot of the monastery. But St Kieran came down from Clonmacnoise and struck his crosier into Phelim's bowels, inflicting a deep wound from which he died. One did not trifle with saints in those days. But it wasn't only lay people who indulged in a spot of plundering in the past. When Clonfert had become a very famous university the monks of far way Cork city became jealous, and they attacked it in the year 807, killing two hundred monks in all, before they were finally repulsed. The most striking feature of the cathedral today is its wonderful west door, with its tall triangular pediment, its six different arches and its wealth of intricate ornamentation of human heads. The pagan Irish of long ago, like the Red Indians, were head hunters. But Christianity adapted this savage custom and civilised it by allowing the substitution of heads of stone for human heads, and the carvings of Clonfert are a perfect example of this sublimation. We were very lucky to see the door at the time of day we did. The afternoon sunlight gives it a great sense of volume and you see it, as it were, on two planes. Embossed on the walls near the high altar are a number of stone carvings, including one of a mermaid whose naked breasts have been polished by the touches of passing hands. Not to be considered singular, the three of us caressed them one after the other and we agreed that it felt quite good. Outside we walked through the headstones and brooding trees which were as silent as the graves themselves. A little doorway led us to the magnificent Yew Tree walk, from the bishop's palace to the church. This has to be seen to be believed. The ancient trees are bent over and form a sheltered arch almost all the way, while the ground underneath feels like a rich oriental carpet, soft and luxurious. The bishop's palace is now a ruin. The last occupant was Sir Oswald Mosley, friend of Hitler and Mussolini, who once hoped that England might turn to dictatorship as a cure for her several ills, but there were many who thought him naive for the good reason, they say, that England was already a dictatorship. In the year 1784, at the height of the penal days there was a decent, honest Protestant bishop of Clonfert, who despaired of converting the Catholics. 'Unable to make the peasants around me good Protestants,' this man of vision said, 'I wish to make them good Catholics, good anything. I have therefore circulated amongst them some of the best of their own authors, whose writings contain much pure Christianity.' The poor man forgot that they could neither speak nor read English, yet his gesture was a magnificent one. How different Irish history would have unfolded itself had there been others like him. The religion of a nation depends upon what its bishops do, not upon what they preach which, for the most part, is little more than light comedy.

We drove back through Banagher and on to Clonony Castle where, in the sixteenth century, a hardy Banagher man took the castle all by himself, killing the three wardens with a hatchet, as well as abducting an attractive woman he found on the premises. But what we really came to see was the grave of the Boylyn family which only came to light in the year 1803. Here they rest, the sisters and cousins of Anne Boylyn. They fled from England, after Henry VIII had her murdered. The same gentleman, who was one of the earliest of the English judicial murderers, died a terrible death, roaring from the pains of syphillis. His break with Rome and his founding of the Protestant Church, ultimately cost the Irish nation over ten million lives. On our way back to the marina we dropped into the Protestant church to the grave of the Reverend Mr Nichols. He was the husband of Charlotte Bronte, and when she died he moved over to Banagher, where he had earlier spent his honeymoon, quite glad, I would imagine, to get away from Haworth parsonage and the craw-thumping hypocritical Mr Bronte.

Before leaving for Shannonbridge we called to Hough's pub for a quick drink. Hough's is one of the many famous pubs on the Shannon that has a special welcome for the river people, like Killeens in Shannonbridge, The Sail Inn in Dromineer, The Merriman Inn in Scarriff, The Jolly Mariner and Sean's Bar in Athlone, The Crews Inn in Roosky and many others. In a corner of the bar we joined a group of Germans who were also cruising and who were fascinated at the decor, and the whole free-and-easy, friendly atmosphere. The continentals had spent the day fishing with some success. 'We've had excellent fishing,' they said. 'But where can we find the lovely Irish girls?' Now if I had known any staid virago in Banagher upon whom I wanted to wreck revenge I would have put them on to her. But I hardly knew a soul. Later I met two very attractive Irish girls who were holidaying in the area and I explained as diplomatically as I could the little problem besetting the Germans, and asked the girls if they would care to join them. Yes, they would. But they wanted it to be clearly understood that they were not going to make dish-clothes or scratching posts of themselves for every randy foreigner-that passed the way. 'They can admire our foliage,' one of the girls whispered in my ear, 'but they won't get near our flowers.'

Back on board we left Banagher and headed upstream to Shannonbridge. Although the afternoon sun was shining brilliantly, a mist was still trailing itself here and there along the surface of the river, and the golden reeds, swishing body high, were nodding and dancing in the gentle breeze. There was a homely, sensuous aroma from the soft green fields of freshly mown hay all along the banks. The course to Shannonbridge, a short distance of an hour or so, is straightforward and well buoyed. We passed the sad lonely entrance to the Grand Canal and the deserted, weed-choked waterway connecting it with Ballinasloe, with all its nostalgic memories of a way of life and a world that is hardly remembered. The beautiful Lehinch Island and the wooded area on the opposite bank was the last green foliage we were to see for quite a while, as we entered great stretches of pathless brown bogland, that go such a long way to supply the nation with fuel and energy. When I gazed across those vast area of brown peat the way of life that is past and gone jumped vividly back to my mind. In my boyhood, when school was over, I had to go to the bog in an ass and cart cut turf, foot it, reek it, save it and then drawn it home for winter fuel. Now one vast conglomeration of machinery does it all and has taken man away from his intimacy with and closeness to the earth. This, of course, is progress and I have supported it all my life, but as I get older, strange confusing thoughts come into my mind and I cannot help wondering if we were not a more fulfilled and contented people when we had to rely on the sweat of our brow. The run from Banagher to Shannonbridge took us just over an hour, so when we came to the little island opposite the River Suck we slipped into the channel behind it and moored to the bank. I would never go up to the village and moor at the quay as long as that infernal Bailey bridge is in position. The noise, clatter and clang as every car passes over it is as deafening as a cannonade. Sleep is impossible and one has to moor, where we did, behind the little island, half-a-mile away. We seem to be able to find millions of pounds for every hairbrained industrial scheme, but we cannot find the few thousands necessary to repair that bridge and bring renewed life to a charming Irish village.* All the same, the delightful walk through fields, hedges, and lush meadows is well worth the extra inconvenience. The remains of the great defences erected to protect the Shannon against an attack from the west are still visible all around the village. There is no doubt about it but Napoleon struck terror into the English occupying army in Ireland, and it was this fear caused them to build those massive defence fortifications here, and at Meelick, Banagher, Athlone and indeed all over the country in the form of Martello towers. Napoleon considered sending an army of 30,000 troops by sea to the west of Ireland and marching across the country to Dublin. One of his best spies at Shannonbridge, a young Irishman named Luke Lawless, sent back a report to Paris to say that Athlone was the only real strong point and that the French army would have no serious trouble taking Banagher or Shannonbridge. However the invasion never came off and when he was in exile on St Helena, Napoleon bitterly regretted that he did not invade Ireland instead of Egypt.

* This has since been remedied

70

He was defeated in 1815 at Waterloo, but because the defence plans had been approved, the British civil service insisted that work on the Shannon fortifications be completed, and so they kept building defences against Napoleon for a year after his exile, until 1816. It has been said that a good civil servant will find a problem in every solution.

Shannonbridge boasts of two renowned sons, Michael McCann and George Brent. Michael McCann was a journalist and newspaper editor, but his most famous composition was the rousing war-song *O'Donnell Aboo*, which has been translated into several languages and is the signature tune of Radio Eireann. Today, nearly one hundred and fifty years after he wrote it, it is one of the most popular songs at concerts and gatherings of musicians. George Brent was born in Shannonbridge, George Nolan, and as a young boy he was one of Michael Collin's trusted IRA dispatch riders. The British offered a large reward for his capture, dead or alive, and he had to flee from Ireland on a fishing trawler to Canada, where he got a job in a theatrical company and eventually made his way to Hollywood and became a world famous film actor as George Brent. He was a matinee idol in the days of Clark Gable, Tyrone Power and Robert Taylor, and starred in over one hundred films before he retired in the fifties. After dinner we strolled up by the river path, through the meadows, past the sad, dilapidated building that once housed the Shannon navigation offices, and on to the end of the village to Killeen's tastefully laid-out hostelry, with its old-world charm. When you go into Killeens you sense immediately an atmosphere of friendship and welcome which at once captures the imagination and gives you the comforting feeling that you are at home. We sat down in a quiet corner, under a signed portrait of George Brent, ordered our drinks, which were served by the dark-haired handsome daughter of the house, Pat Killeen. Later on Pat introduced us to Ned Quigley, a farmer-fisherman, in whose delightful company we spent the rest of the evening. Ned was born on an island in Lough Ree, and for several generations his family made a modest living fishing for eels

71

on the lake but when the government handed this concession over to the ESB most of the fishermen found themselves without a livelihood. Ned is a highly intelligent and observant man, a lover of nature, with a fund of stories and legends about Lough Ree and the River Shannon, which he graciously recalled, until far too soon closing time was upon us and we had to make our way back again through the meadows, to where the boat was berthed.

Early in the morning we started on our journey from Shannonbridge to Athlone which passes through the loneliest and most remote stretch of the Shannon. It is largely inaccessible by road, so that as you pass you see only the fields, pastures, hedges and herds of dreaming cattle chewing the cud. Again the farmhouses are located far back from the river, and are usually built on heights so that they will not be effected by serious flooding which takes place almost every winter. This flooding can at times assume the proportions of a disaster but very little can be done to remedy it. Some years ago a team of experts studied the problem and came up with no real solution because the cost of raising the banks high enough would be far more than land itself is worth. Yet the flooding has some advantages. It waters the fields close to the river and when the floods recede the growth of rich, lush, green grass makes excellent fodder for livestock. When a condescending tourist once questioned a farmer about the flooding he got the reply: 'Ah I don't mind the flooding too much, only at times it becomes annoying when the fish eat the lettuce and gooseberries out of the garden!' When we passed Devenish Island, we saw a group of low hills that looked like little lumps of beauty dropped casually by God. Near them there is a bend in the river, just as you come up to Clonmacnoise, and it has been calculated that this is the mathematical centre of Ireland despite claims to the contrary, which of course means that Shannonbridge has the distinction of being the most central village in Ireland. Landing at Clonmacnoise usually presents slight problems because the jetty

72

is far too small to accommodate more than three or four boats, and normally there are twice or three times that number moored in all positions and at all angles, so one has to do a little skilful manoeuvring to get a berth. However, we managed to tie up alongside a cruiser with French people on board, despite the fact that a young brat kept fishing from the side of the boat until we almost jammed him. We walked up to those wonderful and inspiring ruins and were just in time to join a guided tour conducted by a young archaeological student. Clonmacnoise was founded about 550 by St Ciaran and grew into a university of world renown with more than 4,000 students. Again and again it was attacked and plundered until finally it was looted and burned by English soldiers from Athlone in the twelfth century. This ended its reign of glory. Many of the flat gravestones from the eighth, ninth and tenth centuries, with their epitaphs in Latin and Irish, have been salvaged and are now set into the walls. One of them commemorates the death of the lord abbot in 834. The King of Connaught threw the poor man into the Shannon and drowned him just because he was a Corkman! Flat gravestones were a feature of the early Irish Church and later on upright Celtic crosses became the fashion, but it is quite on the cards that we will return to the flat stones again. In the suburb of an Irish city a new graveyard has recently been opened where no upright crosses are allowed and where flat stones are compulsory. The idea is that upright crosses would disturb commuters to and from the city by reminding them of death. When the conducted tour was over my companions went back to the cruiser to get their cameras, and Maxie and myself continued on through the modern graveyard to the Pilgrim's Road. I wanted to visit the Thieves' Crosses and the Nuns' Church. These three crosses are erected over a mound of stones just outside the walls of Clonmacnoise. It seems as if three gentlemen were executed for highway robbery about the time of Brian Boru and because St Ciaran promised that anyone buried in Clonmacnoise would go straight to heaven, their relatives were anxious that they should be buried within the confines. But the abbot would not hear of it. The relatives then bought a tiny piece of ground outside the boundary and buried the thieves there in the hope that their spirits might be able to hop in over the wall without anyone seeing them and thus get to heaven. Their remains have lain in that lonely grave for over one thousand years and it was only recently that a kind parish priest erected the crosses over their last resting place. No doubt the abbot who refused permission now knows whether he was right or wrong. I walked along the Pilgrim's Road until I came to the Nuns' Chapel with its superb west doorway and chancel arch. This beautiful building was erected in the twelfth century by Dervorgilla as a act of penance for her bohemian life. Dervorgilla, a strikingly beautiful redhead, has been termed the Cleopatra, the Helen of Troy of Ireland. She was given, at an early age, in a loveless marriage to O'Rourke, Prince of Breffini and by all accounts she did not take her marriage vows too seriously. After one of his frequent absences O'Rourke returned home to find his wife gone. Moore's lines commemorate this incident:

> *The valley lay smiling before me*
> *Where lately I left her behind*
> *Yet I trembled and something hung o'er me*
> *That saddened the joy of my mind.*
> *I looked for the lamp which she told me*
> *Would shine when her pilgrim returned*
> *Yet though darkness began to unfold me*
> *No lamp from the battlement burned.*

Dervorgilla had run away with Dermot Mac Murrough, King of Leinster, and to add insult to injury he sent O'Rourke a hundred pieces of gold in payment for his wife. O'Rourke appealed to the high king and they both marched on Dermot who fled to England and sought the help of King Henry. King Henry invaded Ireland and for seven hundred years the fight lasted, costing millions of lives, and all this has been blamed on poor Dervorgilla. Even up to the present day the folk tradition of the people is very hard on her. 'She was a prime bitch,' an old man once told me over a pint. 'There wasn't a prince in the country that she didn't oblige at one time or another, but she wouldn't cushion herself at all for the likes of you nor me because we haven't the blue blood, don't you see. But I do remember one time a journeyman tailor tellin' me that it wasn't altogether her fault. He said her mother brought her up too strict, for she never let her out of her sight and had her at Mass and communion every morning and benediction every evening and 'tis even said that she kept Dervorgilla's legs tied together with the brown scapular until the day she got married. There might be some truth in that because, don't you see, if you don't give children a slack reins now and again they can break out later on and go to the dogs and no bit will ever hold them.' Poor Dervorgilla. The reality is that she was a cultured and sensitive girl forced into a marriage with O'Rourke who was a boor and a scoundrel of the first order. He gave her a terrible life, maltreating and beating her and even going so far as to force her to look on while he was having intercourse with his concubines. She did have the odd night's consolation with a lover when O'Rourke was away plundering and raiding and who would blame her? In the end she got tired of it all and eloped with Mac Murrough. Neither of them were responsible for bringing the English to Ireland. The man responsible for that was Pope Adrian IV who gave his blessing to King Henry and urged him to invade Ireland. Mac Murrough only wanted help from Henry to attack the high king of Ireland and get the throne for himself, which was fairly normal then, and had no idea that Henry was going to invade. But Henry took his son as hostage and tricked Dermot. He then sent Fitzstephens and Fitzgerald, the illegitimate sons by different fathers of his own discarded mistress, at the head of an invading force and Mac Murrough could do nothing to stop them for fear his only son and heir to his throne would be executed forthwith. So the innocent Dervorgilla has had to bear the ignomony of all this. She ended her days in a cloister and gave whatever wealth she had to build and restore churches such as this beautiful one in Clonmacnoise. After the turmoil she found peace:

> *O Earth lie heavily upon her eyes*
> *Seal her sweet eyes weary of watching, Earth,*
> *Lie close around her. Leave no room for mirth*
> *With its harsh laughter nor for sound of sighs*
> *She hath no questions she hath no replies.*

The passage from Clonmacnoise to Athlone, where we planned to stay for the night, takes about two hours. The spacious river winds its way slowly through fertile lands and picturesque countryside, and is probably the most isolated part of this great waterway. There are hardly any roads to be seen and consequently fewer fishermen with their colourful umbrellas. It is a place to woo solitude. Yet the silence is alive. As we cruised along, the tiny wavelets were dancing like jewels in the sun; the lush young reeds were bending over as if to let the summer air pass by. The wild irises spread their golden sheen above the river's edge. Cootes and other waterfowl dashed to and fro towards the sedgy bank. As I lay out on the deck I thought of the song of young love composed so long ago by the Bard of Thomond who fell in love with a girl on the banks of the Shannon:

> *My beautiful Shannon! How oft have I strayed*
> *On thy wild flowery banks with my raven haired maid*
> *And opened my soul to the music that rose*
> *On the sweet fairy wind o'er the summer's repose.*
>
> *'Twas there by the stream flowing brightly along*
> *My spirit inhaled the wild magic of song;*
> *And there mid the calm floral shades of the grove*
> *I first drank the golden enchantment of love.*

For him the Shannon and the quick pain of first love are inseparably linked. It is the same with every one of us. The memory of those places where we first loved, where the touch of a hand awakened our soul, can never grow dim.

The years of sadness and sorrow may tell us that the divine ecstasy of those first thrilling moments has vanished, yet the place where it all happened will never fail to smell of sweet lilac, to bring a thrill of joy to the disillusioned heart. Yet despite the great romantic undertones of human relations I have often wondered if a man can ever be sure of the love of a woman. It is very hard for a poor innocent man to distinguish that which is carefully planned, from that which comes from the heart. Women seem to me to be ruled by unpredictable emotions. They are lovable, loyal, trustful, untrustworthy, lying and treacherous, all at the same time. What they say they mean at the moment, but tomorrow they can say the opposite with equal savagery or equal tenderness, whichever mood their emotional radar tells them is opportune. I have long ago given up. I can understand poor Freud when he said: 'The great question which I have not been able to answer despite my thirty years research into the feminine soul, is: What does a woman want?' They are not only an eternal mystery but a total enigma as well. Yet like the wise man from the east who, having sent his young wife away on the grounds that he could not live with her, brought her back again after a few weeks on the grounds that he could not live without her. Women always win the last battle.

As I lay back on deck enjoying the sunlit silence, broken only by the soft gentle purr of the engine, I flicked through the pages of a helpful little guide to Clonmacnoise and began to speculate on what it must have been like in its hour of glory. In order to minister to the needs of four thousand students at least another two or three thousand people would be necessary; cooks, maids, gardeners, cowhands, butchers, tailors, shoemakers, blacksmiths, teachers, clerks and all kinds of servants to look after every need of the human body and mind. It must then have been as big as a fair-sized town, such as nearby Tullamore or Ballinasloe. Have all these ancilliary buildings vanished without trace? I do not believe it. When Ballintubber Abbey was being restored the excavators found an entire monastery underneath the earth — a monastery whose existence was never suspected. I believe the same could result if Clonmacnoise were properly excavated. Every year the Irish government loses vast sums of the taxpayers' money in bolstering up worthless industries in the vain hope that some miracle will happen, which never does. If they were to spend a tiny fraction of that money excavating and reconstructing Clonmacnoise, it would eventually rank as one of the best investments ever made. Apart from the initial heavy employment content, and the employment of those maintaining it, a reconstructed early Christian university city could become the eighth wonder of the world. It would capture the imagination of all civilised nations and its tourist potential could be counted in millions of pounds each year. But a project like that takes vision and enterprise — two commodities very, very rarely met with in Irish political life. As I read through the little guide I began to consider the whole tragic question of the destruction and plundering of our monasteries. Why should it have happened at all? The answer to that question insofar as the post-sixteenth century period is concerned is simple. The invaders were determined to stamp out the entire Irish race, their religion, their culture, their nationhood and turn the country into a submissive English shire; the destruction of seats of learning and centres of culture was an integral part of that policy. But before that, why were these places looted by our own Irish Christian chieftains? Why did the Danes loot so many of them? The glib answer is that the looters were anti-religious; but this is just not so. The hermits living alone were not interfered with and were let live in peace. The reality contains a very sad truth. They were looted because they were the only places where wealth, gold, silver and precious stones could be found, because many of the followers of Christ in those days were hoarders of wealth. As the centuries passed the teachings of Christ were distorted by the prismatic refractions of human principles; structures became more important than love. The path of material possession very often took precedence over the path of

78

holiness, and many Church leaders went on their knees, not to God but to Mammon, and consequently reaped what was sown. The ruins we see today are, in many cases, not the relics of our inspiration, but the sad harvest of our greed. Yet despite that I passionately believe Clonmacnoise should be restored.

As we drew near to Athlone we began to pick out the multi-coloured sun-shades and umbrellas of the fishermen all along the banks. There were scores of them on both sides for nearly a mile below the town, sitting there patiently, some reading, some dozing, but all waiting for the magic moment when a fish would bite. Under one umbrella set close to the ground I saw a youth tenderly making love to a pretty girl, gently caressing her hair and rapturously kissing her, oblivious to the noise of our engine or indeed to the violent bobbing of his cork in the water. I was tempted to sound the horn to bring him back to reality, but I remembered I was once young myself and so I left him in his seventh heaven:

> *I loved her with a burning love*
> *That matched my boyhood well*
> *And brilliant were the dreams I wove*
> *While tranced in that sweet spell;*
> *And in my breast she'll reign and rest*
> *Each eve while sad I pore,*
> *Where ferns are green the rocks between,*
> *And shiver the red lushmore.*

When we arrived at the lock, luck was with us as the lower gates were just opening so we had no delay and very quickly we were through and tied up to a barge alongside the quay, a short distance upstream. It wasn't bad at all to hear the throb of human life again after the long hushed silence of the river.

4

After lunch my two companions had to leave and catch a train to Dublin so I was once more alone with Maxie; but it was not to be for long. My son Gerald and my daughter Mary would be joining me that night and would accompany me for the remainder of the cruise. When my companions had gone I let go the ropes and motored out to the 'Jolly Mariner' marina about half-a-mile further upstream. At any time the 'Jolly Mariner' is a delightful berth but today there was a more pragmatic reason why I made the move. It was to avoid the activities of the young thieves of Athlone who specialise in stealing radios, binoculars, cameras, fishing rods and even bicycles. The decent people of the town rightly abhor this but there is little they can do about it, even though it must affect their business quite a lot. Once before, when I was tied up at the quays, I caught one of these youngsters trying to steal a fishing rod from the boat. I quickly decided that to call the police would be a waste of time so I took the law into my own hands and gave him a couple of good clips under the ear and a hard boot in the behind which sent him scampering away. This I believe to be the most effective way of dealing with these young Bugsie Malones. If you have them brought to court some psychologist may give evidence that they had deep-rooted pre-natal reactions, according to Dr Freud, and they will probably get away with it. At least I know if the fellow I punished ever sees me again on the quays of Athlone I feel sure he will realise in a flash that I have no great sympathy with the modern psychological approach to juvenile delinquency and I imagine he will react accordingly. The 'Jolly Mariner' marina is owned by *Athlone Cruisers Ltd.*, a firm of the very highest international standards and run by its helpful founder, Kerry Sloane. For people cruising the

Shannon this is a home from home. There is a wonderful restaurant and bar on the marina itself and the staff of both places are amongst the friendliest and most helpful. I found a vacant berth and with a little tricky manoeuvring I made fast. I put Maxie on the lead and set out to explore Athlone, visit the bookshops, look at some prominent buildings and do a little shopping. It is always a trifle embarrassing to go shopping with Maxie because of the number of establishments who display notices *No Dogs Allowed*. I suppose they have their reasons but I would much prefer to see the kind of notice that one can see displayed in a well-known continental hotel: *Of course your dog is welcome. In our long experience of the hotel business no dog has ever stolen our linen and towels, no dog has broken our glasses in a drunken brawl, no dog has ever tried to seduce our female staff, no dog has ever passed a dud cheque on us. If you can guarantee yourself to be as well behaved as your dog, you too are welcome.*

Athlone is a very cultured town. It has an active historical society who publish the excellent *Journal of the Old Athlone Society*. It is the venue for one of the biggest drama festivals in Europe and the average citizen has a more than ordinary discernment for Irish literature, painting and sculpture. I suppose the spirit of a place with a great past lives on, and Athlone had a great past. They say it got its name from an enterprising gentleman named Luan who lived in the first century. The Shannon was fordable here and Luan saw the possibilities of having a good clean pub and eating house where weary and tired customers would have to pass. So he opened up his hostelry at the ford, and by all accounts he did well, having built up a reputation for good food and drink and what more could any traveller ask for in those far-off days — and I am sure he did not forbid dogs. The place then became known as Ath Luain, The Ford of Luan. Of course later on they built a bridge and I presume Luan's descendants were enterprising enough to see the new opportunities although there were times in the history of Athlone when it would pay a cautious businessman to keep well away from that same crossing. That bridge, which was further downstream, was finally demolished and the present one built in its place. The old bridge had a delightful carving which luckily was saved and is now preserved in the National Museum. The carving depicted one, Peter Lewis, having in his hand a pistol and on the pistol a rat. The story goes that Lewis was an English Catholic monk who turned Protestant. Ever after that he was haunted by a Catholic rat who followed him everywhere even to bed, and when the poor man sat at the table the rat annoyed him by dipping his whiskers into the wine. Lewis was a man of great scientific and engineering knowledge and he was sent to help construct the bridge at Athlone. He also preached occasionally in the Protestant church and one day when he was delivering himself of a sermon in the pulpit the rat appeared in front of him on the pedestal. This was too much for Lewis so he produced a pistol to put an end to the animal who, however, jumped up on the pistol and gave the unfortunate man such a bit on the thumb that he died of lock-jaw — a warning to preachers not to bring pistols into pulpits. One house in Athlone I was particularly anxious to see was that of a gentleman called Will Handcock who represented Athlone in parliament, but unfortunately no one could tell me for certain where it was. In 1798 Will sang the most rabid anti-British and anti-union songs at the great municipal dinner but, being a first rate politician, he saw what way the wind was blowing, and in 1800 at the same function he sang the most pro-British and pro-union songs. He afterwards voted for the Union for which Lord Castlereagh gave a generous cash settlement and had Will created Viscount Castlemaine. The same Lord Castlereagh was a much hated man in Ireland, and it seems he was not too well liked in England either if one is to judge by the epitaph Byron wrote when he died:

> *Posterity shall ne'er behold*
> *A nobler grave than this*
> *Here lie the bones of Castlereagh*
> *Pause, traveller, and p———.*

As I walked over the historic bridge of Athlone towards the old castle my mind turned on its last fatal siege and the sad consequences that followed. This terrible war had little to do with Irish freedom — it was merely a bloody struggle for power between two kings for the throne of England; the useless James II and the able, ruthless William of Orange, who incidentally was married to James' daughter, a renowned bigot who hated her father and all he represented. The Irish believed that James II would restore their lands and give them freedom to practise their religion and so, like in World War I and World War II, thousands of trusting Irish gave their lives for what eventually turned out to be just absolutely nothing. Since the French were helping, the king of that country put his own general in command of the anti-Williamite forces in Ireland. This was a major error of judgment. The only first-class general on the Irish side was Patrick Sarsfield, a man rightly feared by King William and his higher staff, but Sarsfield was relegated to a minor command. The man chosen was the Frenchman, General St Ruth, who by any standards was a most odd choice. He was a man of extremely ugly appearance with little ability. The only reputation he had in France was that of a Protestant persecutor and a wife beater. Many contemporary sources say that he was sent to Ireland because King Louis wanted him out of France as he was paying undue attention to the queen. This was the man upon whom all Irish hope was pinned. The brilliant General de Ginkel, who commanded the Williamite forces, failed to cross the bridge, due entirely to the bravery of Sergeant Costume and a section of Irish troops, and after eight fruitless days attacking he withdrew, but on the ninth day he succeeded in effecting a crossing at an unguarded ford further down river. It is said that General St Ruth with some of his French staff, were in their quarters drinking heavily and whooping it up with a group of Irish prostitutes at the moment the break-through occurred. It must have been an intriguing kind of an evening's fun because the ladies spoke only Irish and St Ruth and his friends only French. But I suppose the language of what was engaging the attention of the revellers is international and one can reasonably assume no major difficulties attended the final objectives. When it ultimately dawned on St Ruth that Ginkel had really broken through he retreated to another defence line at Aughrim. Here again he kept not only Sarsfield in the dark but also his own second-in-command and his French staff officers, so that no one really knew what his plans were. Ginkel attacked and during the battle St Ruth arrogantly insisted on riding his white charger all over the place, making himself a perfect target for any sniper. As always there was an Irishman ready to sell the pass. An Aughrim sheep farmer named Kelly pointed St Ruth out in the distance to Ginkel's men. They fired on him with cannon and the third ball blew off his head. As none of his staff knew what his plans were or how his various regiments were disposed the whole army went into total disarray and Ginkel's troops simply mowed them down. Worse still, Henry Luttrell, who commanded an important part of the Irish cavalry, deserted and went over to Ginkel having surrendered his troops. This put an end to all Irish resistance. A few years later some survivors of the battle searched out Luttrell and found him being borne in luxury in a sedan chair through a Dublin street. They promptly took him out and shot him dead. Luttrell was so hated for this act of treachery that long afterwards his body was removed from the grave and his skull smashed to pieces with a pick-axe. Between ten and fifteen thousand Irish bodies lay strewn around the battlefield of Aughrim, including over a hundred priests who, during the battle, ran through the lines with crucifixes urging the soldiers to fight for their religion. There was nobody to bury the Irish dead. Their bodies were scattered for miles over the countryside, decaying and disintegrating, torn to pieces by hundreds of marauding dogs, rats, carrion and all types of vermin. One Irish officer who was killed had his wolfhound with him, and the dog kept guard for many months over his master's crumbling remains, savagely attacking any animal or man that tried to come near it. In Athlone the English command heard of this faithful Irish dog and, fearing that the incident would capture the imagination of the people and become a folk-saga, they sent out a section of troops who shot the loyal wolfhound dead and left him to rot with his master. But he was not entirely forgotten. An Irish ballad, still sung in the pubs commemorates the incident:

When Saxon fiends the scene of death and robbery had fled
An Irish wolfhound sought his lord mid heaps of pilfered
    dead
And strove with more than human love to rob death of its
    prize
Then moaned a dirge above his breast and licked his lips
    and eyes.

When autumn pencilled summer's bloom in tints of gold
    and red
And winter over hill and dale a ghostly mantle spread
The weird winds blew across the moor and moaned down
    the dell
Yet guarded well that noble dog his master where he fell.

Spring timidly was glancing down upon the spreading plain
Where those long months in loneliness the faithful dog had
    lain
When tramping loud across the moor the English soliders
    trod
And halted 'neath the only bones remaining on the sod.

Up sprang the faithful wolfhound he knew a foe was near
And feared that foe would desecrate the bones he loved so
    dear
Fierce and defiant there he stood; the soldiers seized with
    dread
Took aim and fired—the noble dog fell on his master—dead.

Today in Aughrim there is a memorial to St Ruth. It would be more appropriate if that memorial commemorated the devotion and fidelity, loyalty and love of an Irish wolf-hound.

I rambled back through the town and went browsing in the bookshops. Here again I found out that Irish paperbacks outsell foreign ones, especially to British tourists who are prevented in their own country by the most powerful censorship in the world from learning anything about Ireland except what is degrading and discreditable. I went into the Athlone tourist office with a few queries and I found the staff there most helpful and ready to go to any trouble to answer my questions and give me the information I was seeking. I later dropped in to the spacious cathedral overlooking the river and sat down in a pew near the high altar. I was alone except for an old woman with a sad but dignified face who was doing the stations of the cross, her rosary interlaced through her waxen fingers. The silence of the great edifice breathed a kind of holy tranquillity that could easily inspire even an atheist to pray. I remained there just a few minutes in thoughtless meditation, at peace with myself and with the world. On my way out I had a look at the Italian statues, much criticised by so many writers, but I could see nothing very wrong with them. Many sophisticated critics forget that the ordinary, suffering, simple people can find great consolation and inspiration in these works. Truth is essential to life; great art is not; and what passes for great art in many of our modern churches can at times be positively revolting. On the way back to the marina I called in to an attractive, pleasing delicatessen where I spent more than half-an-hour loading myself with the most delightful and appetising foods. Back at the 'Jolly Mariner' I got on board and went into the cabin for what I hoped would be a short nap. But I slept till well past eight o'clock and was awakened only by the arrival of Mary and Gerald, tired from their long journey. After dinner we crossed to the tasteful 'Jolly Mariner' bar and as so often happens we found ourselves in the company of a delightful Dutch couple who were, like ourselves, cruising the Shannon.

When one strikes up an acquaintance with continentals the conversation generally turns on Ireland and the Irish and this evening was no exception. The Dutch couple were spending their fifth holiday here. Usually they spent a week on the Shannon and then three weeks touring around by car. It did not take me long to find out that they had a deep and extensive knowledge of Ireland and had read widely on matters pertaining to our history, politics and culture. Later when they believed they had sized me up and when the drink loosened tongues a bit the man explained that he had a very serious question to ask and he hoped I would not be offended by what he had to say. 'I know Ireland fairly well,' he said, 'but there is one mystery which I have never been able to solve and which I have been slow to talk about lest I give offence. I cannot comprehend what it is that makes the Irish seem so servile. What I mean is, that all through the country we have been virtually unable to buy Irish goods. In the supermarkets eighty to ninety percent of the goods for sale are foreign and I know that these commodities are made and can be made in Ireland. In one town I had to try three shops before I could get Irish biscuits. If that kind of thing happened on the continent the wives of the trade-unionists would boycott those shops and in no time they would be forced to close. If seems as if the Irish trade-unionists think only of going on strike. They never seem to see that they have a positive role in regard to Irish-made goods. I noticed that the boats on the Shannon, for which there is a substantial government grant available are almost all foreign made, while your boat-yards are closing down. Even the delph on most of the boats is foreign yet I read recently that hundreds of pottery workers are being made redundant. Again, on a different level, I notice your media will always give exposure to the foreigner in preference to the Irishman, even though the foreigner be third-class and the Irishman first-class. I noticed some time ago when the results of one of your general elections came out British television passed it off in a few moments despite the millions of Irish in England

87

who were deeply interested in these results. Yet when there was a British general election your television devoted a large part of the evening to it when it would appear to me that only a handful of people in Ireland were interested. What is the answer to this enigma? I always thought the Irish were a proud, self-respecting race, but I am forced to the conclusion, and I say this without offence, that this is far from being so. Are you still a nation of forelock-lifters and toadies?'

His thesis seemed unanswerable. I had no facts or figures to counter them, and it seemed to me as if a substantial part of what he said was true. I could only try to explain. I told him that for hundreds of years we were beaten into pulp, treated as animals, and then suddenly we got our freedom. We were simply not able for it. It was somewhat like as if you planted a sally tree and bent over its top and tied it in a loop to the ground, and then after twenty years cut the string. The loop would gradually straighten but it would take several years before it would be upright again. We as a nation are like that tree. We are still partly on all fours. We still wear the invisible badge of slavery. It will take another generation or two before we are mature enough to stand on our own feet and declare ourselves Irish.

He was not very deeply impressed by what I had to say and the discussion continued backwards and forwards for the rest of the evening until closing time. As we were saying good night he asked me if the ordinary Irishman was ashamed to go into a shop and demand Irish-made goods. I had to admit that this was so. 'Then,' he said, 'the sooner you rejoin the empire and bow to the queen the better. Good night.' What he had said was a bitter pill to swallow but most of it was true. I only wished I could have answered him effectively. The indomitable spirit of all the Irish is one of our pathetic fictions. It was only the few who possessed this spirit, who defeated an empire, who made the world sit up and take notice. The majority did very little. They were so long slaves that they had come to love their masters.

Next morning we headed upstream towards the lovely Lough Ree, and as we moved along I remembered a delightful love story connected with the admiralty chart of the lake. It is generally recognised that the chart of Lough Ree is far more detailed and more accurate than the Lough Derg chart. The reason is that Lieutenant R. B. Beechy, who surveyed the lakes, was doing a strong line with a Miss Smith of Portlick, on the shores of Lough Ree. It was therefore natural that he should pay special attention to these waters, and so this chart is much more detailed. The story had a happy ending and he eventually married her. Lough Ree was looking its very best as its calm shadowless waters opened up before us. Today it was hard to realise that even a moderate wind, rising suddenly, could lash this peaceful lake into a wild fury and build up short steep seas, positively dangerous to any craft. Like a beautiful woman, it is treacherous and should never be trusted except in the most settled weather.

We planned to go straight for Lanesboro with just one short stop at Inish Clearann. As we moved out into the lake we passed several small islets, including the beautiful wooded Hare Island, once the secret headquarters of the Fenians. Farther in on the mainland lived a delightful character in the last century called Bevan Slator. Bevan was the eccentric owner of the Ballymahon flour mills and had a soft spot for cats. He kept hundreds of them ruled over by a master tom-cat called Tom Fidly. Tom was responsible for the good conduct of all the other cats and if he failed to keep them in order he was put on short rations and in solitary confinement. Another delightful eccentric who lived near this area was Adolphus Cooke, who remodelled his large mansion making the doors and windows arched to go with his dining room chairs. He wore yellow stockings and had his coach repainted to go with them also. When his father died Adolphus believed that he was reincarnated in a large turkey-cock and he gave strict instructions to all his male workers, to raise their hats when they passed the cock, and to his female workers, to curtsey. Once when the lodgekeeper let in unwelcome visitors to the estate Cooke punished him by ordering him to get rid of his wife and take another. He hated children, and many of the tenants on his estate had to hide their children in case they would be evicted. Once a local farmer sought help on the grounds that he had twelve mouths to feed but Cooke told him to be gone with himself because he had been a very mischievous man, while at the same time he gave five pounds to a tinker who told him he had no children. Another eccentric of a more sinister kind, a British officer, Lieutenant Hempenstall, left a trail of blood and tears after him throughout the countryside around Lough Ree. Hempenstall was known as the 'Walking Gallows'. He was a very tall man and he perfected an art of hanging low sized Irishmen or women by taking off his silk scarf, tying it around the person's neck and jumping up and down laughing with glee until the victim was dead. He roamed the countryside and took a keen delight in flogging to death any Irishman he happened to meet. His speciality was taking little children from their mothers' arms and battering them to death in front of their screaming parents. He rarely missed a fair, where he would discreetly watch the farmers and as they held out their hands to clinch a deal he would draw his sword and cut them off at the wrist. Once he drove into the village of Moyvore in a horse-and-cart which contained so many mutilated corpses that their intestines were trailing along the ground. Then for fun he burned every house in the village while he himself and his troops sang hymns in praise of King George. When he died some wag wrote on the wall of the churchyard:

Here lie the bones of Hempenstall
Judge, jury, gallows, rope and all.

Before he died Hempenstall was presented with a specially engraved silver plate by the gentlemen of the county for his services to King George.

We passed the wooded Rindoon Point where Turgesius, King of the Danes, had his castle from which he controlled Lough Ree until Brian Boru put an end to his occupation by raising a fleet and attacking him from the water as well as from the land. Local tradition has it that when the Danes sacked Clonmacnoise they gave the father-and-mother of a party that night at which Turgesius' wife did the dance of the seven veils on the high altar, and afterwards used the sacred vessels to pour wine over her naked body before seducing three brawny Danish officers. Poor Turgesius was plastered drunk all the time, snoring his head off on top of the tomb of a high king of Ireland.

When we arrived at Inish Clearann the mooring buoy was occupied so we had to throw out an anchor. I always take the precaution of bringing along a fisherman anchor as I find it holds much better than other types on the pebbly slippery bottom of a lake. Mary and Gerald stayed on board in case a wind blew up and the boat needed extra attention, while Maxie and myself made our way in the punt to the little landing slip. Inish Clearann is a dream island, one of those places where you instinctively feel you belong and where you have the wild desire to spend the rest of your days until the end of time. As I strolled up through the lush grass I sensed a peace as if the fragrant atmosphere of prayer was lingering across the centuries. The old ruins, covered in ivy, cast haunting shadows on the soft grass. It could have been the tenth century and not the twentieth. Like Inishcealtra, there is a Church of the Dead where the sombre chant of the *De Profundis* bade a last goodbye to hundreds of monks whose lives were dedicated to service of their fellow-man. There is the diminutive Tempall Diarmada where a monk in deep sorrow or tormented by doubts could speak alone with God. Tempall Mor had a refectory and a chapter room where all brethren prostrated themselves once a week and publicly confessed their faults. These were great men by any standards. They gave up the pleasures and joys of this world so that they might love God more and inspire their fellow human beings. They suffered a great deal from superiors who, for the most part, were politically minded humbugs whose hearts were securely anchored on this earth. Our judgment of these worldly bishops and abbots must always be tempered by the thought that there were thousands of ordinary monks who willingly suffered the most terrible privations and who died nameless and unknown. But to any reflective traveller, who sees in a monastery more than stone walls, the lives of these heroic monks could not be in vain. I did not go to Tempall Clogas as it is away on the other side but on my way back I looked at the ruins of Fairbrother's cottage. Fairbrother was an ignoramus of the last century who desecrated the churches by using the stones to build a farmhouse for himself. But the spirit that rules such places cast a spell on his cattle and they ran in a wild frenzy all over the island many of them plunging into the lake and drowning. Fairbrother took the hint and left for the mainland.

As I made my way back I thought of the many lovely stories about Lough Ree that Ned Quigley told me in Shannonbridge. Ned grew up amongst the islands and as a child he heard the old people telling stories by the turf fires at night, and like a true artist he recorded them as he heard them. One concerned a wake on Inish Clearann. At some-time during the night a frog jumped out of the corpse's mouth and into the ashes. That was a sign that the soul was gone to Purgatory. If the frog jumped into the fire it would be a sign the soul was gone to hell. Another concerned Cromwell's visit to Inishbofin. There was a carving of a bishop on the gable end of the church and Cromwell did not like it so he took up his revolver, aimed and fired. He cut the top off the bishop's nose but ever after that the eye he closed when taking aim remained shut. One of the old fishermen saw him hundreds of years later and, although he had by then grown a white goatee beard and was smoking a turned-down pipe, the eye was still shut. He seemed a decent inoffensive sort of a man, the fisherman said. Ned heard other stories about the devil in the form of a black cat, headless men in boats, the murder of hundreds of nuns on one island, and many more. One of the most interesting things he told me, which was not a folk tale, concerned the mode of transport when the lake was frozen over. Two men would put a ladder flat on the ice. A man would sit on one end and the second man on the other end. Each would have a pitch fork and would ski their way to the mainland.

As we moved up towards Lanesboro I felt a trifle disappointed that the terms of my charter did not allow me to visit Inny Bay and the Inny River — because of navigational problems these are out of bounds to hired boats. My interest in the Inny lies in the fact that one of my favourite poets, John Keegan Casey was born near its banks and wrote so much about it. Few of the millions of music lovers who heard the world's greatest tenors sing *Maire My Girl* ever knew that Casey composed it.

> *Over the dim blue hills*
> *Strays a wild river*
> *Over the dim blue hills*
> *Rest my heart ever*
> *Dearer and brighter than*
> *Jewels and pearl*
> *Dwells she in beauty there*
> *Maire my girl.*
>
> *Down upon Claris heath*
> *Shines the soft berry*
> *On the brown harvest tree*
> *Droops the red cherry*
> *Sweeter thy honey lips*
> *Softer the curl*
> *Straying adown thy cheeks*
> *Maire my girl.*
>
> *'Twas on an April eve*
> *That I first met her*
> *Many an eve shall pass*
> *Ere I forget her*
> *Since my young heart has been*
> *Wrapped in a whirl*
> *Thinking and dreaming of*
> *Maire my girl.*

Casey was born in Gurteen in 1846 and twenty-four years later he died. His poems and songs made such an impact on the country that more than fifty thousand people followed his remains to Glasnevin cemetery. He was also a wanted man. He spent a term in jail and most of his short life he was on the run from British intelligence agents. When Ireland was at its lowest ebb he threw his lot in with the people and his poetry and songs gave expression to their sufferings, sorrows and aspirations. The guns of the men who persecuted him are silent, their swords rusted, their names forgotten, but Casey's poetry and melodies live on. In 1869, the year before he died, his first volume of one hundred poems appeared. Casey may truly be termed Westmeath's greatest Irish poet. Some would claim this distinction for Oliver Goldsmith but I think that claim is unreal. A lot of people claim they are Irish simply because they happen to be born here. This claim is, of course, totally spurious. An Irishman is one who is absolutely committed to Ireland, its people, its language, its culture and who is prepared to lay down his life, if necessary, to this cause. Goldsmith was born in Westmeath by an accident of birth, but unlike Casey, he spent most of his life in England and gave his loyalties to that country. *The Deserted Village* is a poem of the English countryside and I cannot see that it is in any way typical of an Irish village. At that time the population of Westmeath spoke only Irish so Goldsmith would not have understood a word of what they were saying. The penal laws were in full swing so there could be no noisy school house so charmingly described by Goldsmith. Ninety-five percent of the population had to attend illegal hedge schools, and run the risk of transportation if they were caught. There was a price on every schoolmaster's head. The beautiful hawthorn bush with seats beneath the shade and the whole village happy all around it was perfectly true of an English village but it was a complete myth as far as Westmeath was concerned. Lieutenant Hempenstall and his equals were on the rampage at that time and God help any Irishman who tried to voice his opinion on any village green. Goldsmith was, of course, a great poet, but a great English poet, who wrote his most famous poem entirely, I believe, about an English village and about the people of the English countryside, with perhaps the odd flash-back to his youth. All the same, one cannot be too hard on local enthusiasts who, in the interests of tourism, point out all the places mentioned in *The Deserted Village*. After all if one examined the bible with a little ingenuity one could claim that most of the places mentioned were in West Cork!

Soon we were moving through Ballyclare Cut which is the gateway to Lanesboro. As is nearly always the case the wharf was crowded but by a little skilful manoeuvring we found a space at the entrance to the small harbour and there we berthed for lunch. After our meal we went for a short stroll through the village, across the bridge where two provinces, two counties, and two dioceses meet, up to the church with the graves of its priests in military formation, and back down the other side to where a new marina is being built. Lanesboro is a very clean town with good shops and above all, a friendly and helpful people, particularly the chemist, whom I know from past experience will open his shop outside business hours to help someone in need of medicaments.

The last time I was in Lanesboro I met a most unusual Englishman whose hobby was studying animal and reptile life. I spent a delightful evening with him while he talked non-stop about their habits and idiosyncrasies. But he had me literally roaring with laughter when he launched out on a description of their love life. 'Animals were more honest than human beings,' he said, 'since they were willing to perform no matter who was looking. Did you know,' he said, 'that the ordinary ram is a frolicksome devil when the feeling comes over him? He can make up to a hundred performances in one day and keep that up for the best part of a month. The bull, if he is put to it, can oblige sixty times a day. Boars aren't so good. They can only transact four times a day. Worms are real sex maniacs. When the male enters the female she holds him there for a month and they keep twisting and turning, and moaning, and sighing until they are covered in a ball of froth, and they never stop for thirty days. Frogs are as queer as hell. In the mating season the male frog grows spikes on his hands so that he can grip the slippery female, but he's kind of stupid because when the feeling is on him he'll tackle anything, a gosling, a lizard, a mouse, a chicken or even a sod of turf if its wet. I spent years trying to figure out how hedgehogs did it. I always thought it could be somewhat awkward with the spikes, and then one day I saw two of them, of all places in a graveyard, behind a headstone. It was really quite simple. The female just flattened her spikes till her whole back was as smooth as silk and the male slipped into position while you'd be winking your eye. The barnacle's organ is nearly thirty times longer than his body and at night when there are a lot of them crowded together he slips it out and lets it wander around the colony until he finds a female willing to take it. But the strangest of all is the snail, and I think 'tis very unfair that they have the best of both worlds. Each snail has a male and female organ so that when they are mating each one of them gets two thrills. The two organs are side by side behind the ear so if you ever see two snails starting to rub their heads together you'll know it isn't just dandruff that's troubling them.' I learned of the gymnastics of elephants, kangaroos, giraffes, crocodiles, hyennas, snakes and almost every kind of animal and reptile, and by the time he was finished my respect for their imaginative ingenuity far exceeded that of humans. When we parted he gave me his address and invited me to call on him to see his vast library on his strange hobby and I do hope that one day I will be able to do so.

This tiny harbour at Lanesboro is another of those secret places on the Shannon so full of memories of the past. Here the bargemen of old rested, sometimes for days, while waiting for the wild waters of Lough Ree to calm. They busied themselves cleaning their decks, making minor repairs and passing on the latest lore and gossip of the river to the locals. Their place has now been taken by tourists, the harbour has been renovated and there are dirt recepticles all around to meet the needs of our present-day pollution, but it has never lost its character, charm and old-worldiness and just to meander along its rough hewn stones is to touch a past that is slowly becoming a memory.

After Lanesboro a great variety begins to unfold over the countryside. There are more trees and woodland patches, more hills, more farmhouses close to the banks, more plantations, like the strange line of feathery popular trees a few miles upstream. There is a story told explaining the sudden appearance of so many trees after Lanesboro. It is said that an eccentric priest of the last century, a lover of woodland, was largely responsible. When a man confessed to him that he had committed adultery the priest gave him the penance of planting a new tree on the banks of the Shannon. The person who told me the story felt that this idea should be taken up by the Department of Forestry and the Irish hierarchy. He felt that such co-operation could result in the reafforestation of the whole country within a decade.

As we sailed along in the beautiful sunshine the poetry of the earth was everywhere around us. In the fields the cows stood staring and listening to life singing in the grass; little playful rabbits fringed the hedges; on a far-off wind-swept ledge a lone horse silhouetted against the sky; scarecrows in the tillage with outstretched arms, looked like politicians at election time; the hue of the heather on distant Slieve Bawn changing with every light; the sedge bowing before a soft wind and mingling with the sunbeams dancing on the water; overhead the cry of the curlews suspended in the sky. The air was alive with the joy of the earth. Round every bend in the river here there is something new:

I will remember with sad heart next year
This music and this water, but today
Let me be part of all this joy. My ear

97

Caught far off melodies I hid away.
The light of one fair face that fair would stay,
Upon my heart's broad canvas.

When we arrived at Termonbarry Lock good fortune was once again with us. The lower gates were open and in a short time the genial, ever helpful, Tom Feeney saw us through. Tom is one of the most co-operative lock-keepers on the Shannon. He has a smile, a greeting and a bit of useful advice for everyone. A lock-keeper's job is one I do not envy. He spends most of his day turning the huge keys and pushing the gates open and shut; but perhaps the most exasperating thing of all is having to deal with inexperienced boat crews who do not know one end of a rope from the other. Yet all the Shannon lock-keepers have the reputation of being courteous and helpful, particularly to the inexperienced. They have a most responsible job that cannot be rushed, and in these days of hurry and haste this is something that is well to remember and indeed admire. There is a story told of an impatient, smart-alec foreigner who, in an attempt to be clever, asked a lock-keeper if he could speak Irish. The lock-keeper said he could. 'Tell me,' said the foreigner, 'is there any word in the Irish language that corresponds with the South American word "manyana"?' The lock-keeper thought for a moment. 'No,' he replied, 'there is not. We have no word in the Irish language that expresses such a strong sense of urgency!' And he continued with his work.

Termonbarry is another of the many restful, green-bordered berthing places one finds on the Shannon. Above the lock there are two wharfs, both conveniently laid out beside a tree-lined river walk of rustic charm. We made fast to one and relaxed in the peaceful atmosphere of this delightful little village. After a cup of coffee, Gerald went fishing. Mary lay in the sunshine and Maxie and myself rambled up towards the village. In the sixth century St Barry founded a monastery here, which became possibly the first mental home in Ireland. When he was searching for a site he wanted to cross Lough Forbes, but unfortunately, he had no boat. There was a huge rock nearby and using his saintly powers he turned it into a boat and crossed the lake. This stone craft can still be seen at the Catholic church in nearby Whitehall so I thought I might take a stroll over that way to have a look at it. But just as I reached the road a large automobile flashed past and then came suddenly to a halt a short distance away. I could see a hand waving at me. I walked quickly up to where the car was stopped and recognised a very old acquaintance. Now this man has always been something of an enigma to me. I had known him as a student and had run into him occasionally over the years. I knew him to be a practical joker as well as a talent-ed magician who could make things seemingly appear and disappear at will. But whenever I met him he always claim-ed he was a professional pickpocket and that this was his sole means of livelihood. I never really knew whether or not he was pulling my leg. People in any way connected with writing are always a fair target for practical jokers. Stories and incidents are often discreetly planted in the hope that they may be published and later turn out to be hoaxes. One of the classic cases concerns the reader who writes to a country newspaper saying he has dug up an antique urn thousands of years old with the following inscription: ITI . . . SAPIS . . . SPOT. . ; could any kind reader decipher it etc. Usually after publication the unfortunate editor finds out too late that by rearranging the letters the inscription reads: IT IS A PISS POT. So when we had adjourned to a pub I put on my best poker face and asked my friend how things were in the pickpocketing business not really know-ing whether I would believe a word he was going to say.

'Times have changed at lot,' he replied. 'I have to put a great deal more thought into my work nowadays. Indeed I attended a special course on the principles of small business management and by putting these principles into action, I increased my income several fold. For example, I found out that wise men can learn a lot more from fools than fools can from wise men. I also learned the value of market research in my profession. A hard realistic exercise in market research taught me where to find the money. The old seedy type of pickpocket at the racecourse still lingers on but it has had its day. Race meetings today are attended mostly by people who operate on credit so there is little loose cash in their pockets. Depending on the racecourse is like a farmer trying to fatten geese on a bog where you couldn't feed a snipe. My market research taught me to pay attention to the rich workers, the well-heeled kind who strike at a moment's notice. Wherever they gather you will find me not far away. Some time ago a group of these refused to handle a consignment of lavatories unless they got an extra fifty pounds per man embarrassment money. They got what they wanted and I was promptly on the spot the evening they were paid. While they were celebrating with pints I removed a hundred pounds from their pockets in the space of one hour. I'm sure you've often seen tinkers who deal in antiques. Well some of them are very wealthy and can have up to a thousand pounds in their caravans. I stroll amongst them, where they are congregated on a site, pretending to buy antiques, and rarely fail to depart without being well rewarded. The religious field is quite lucrative too. I attend as many charismatic meetings as I can and when the women are holding hands and singing with their eyes turned towards heaven 'tis a simple matter to attend to their purses. But pilgrimages and shrines produce most of all. I visit Knock twice or three times a year and each visit is worth a few hundred pounds to me. Of course, at Knock and places like that I usually put an Ash-Wednesday look on my face. This makes lifting the wallets much easier. There's a rumour the Pope is going to visit Knock and I'm very much looking forward to that visit. It should net me a good haul.'

'Do you not think it a bit blasphemous to be lifting money at places like Knock,' I asked. 'Not in the least,' he replied promptly. 'I never interfere with the invalids but I regard all others as fair game. The majority go there either out of superstitious curiosity or out of a sense of selfishness looking for a divine handout. I am too long in the world now to judge a man by the size of his prayer book. To me all these self-seekers are fair game. I always take the ball on the first hop in case it would burst on the second. Religion is a multi-million pound business in the first place and a means of salvation in the second. Let me try to explain it theologically to you.' I think when he was young he was a candidate for the priesthood and more than once before I had listened in awe to his theological justifications for his pursuits. 'Look at the Mass,' he continued with a profound and almost angelic look on his face. 'In the Mass Christ dies again for mankind the same as he did on Calvary. Because Christ was God any merit he generates is infinite. Therefore, the merits of the Mass are infinite. But the merits of two Masses or three Masses cannot be more infinite than the merits of one. On the fallacy that they can, billions of pounds change hands every year, and no cleric will explain the true theological reality, and small blame to them. A turkey never voted for an early Christmas. The few thousands I help myself to is trifling. Believe me if I'm rammed in for all eternity I'll sure have plenty of company, and it won't be all pickpockets.'

'Since you spoke about the Mass,' I asked trying to suppress the laughter, 'is it long since you've been there?' ''Tis so long since I've been to Mass now,' he replied, 'that God would have to look through a telescope to find me.' We chatted for about half an hour on the dishonesty of workers, the imorality of tax evasion and other such kindred subjects. Then he explained to me that he had an urgent appointment at a large confraternity rally and was in a bit of a hurry so we quickly finished our drinks and left the pub. The car jumped off to a start but when he had gone about fifty yards he stopped and called me. I ran up as he turned down the window. 'You must have mislaid this,' he said and then drove off hurriedly. It was my wallet. I checked it carefully. There was nothing missing. But in it I found a small card which I had never seen before and which was certainly not in my wallet the last time I opened it. Neatly printed on one side of the card were the famous words of Barnum: *There's a fool born every minute and most of them live*; and printed on the other side a quotation from the Gospels: *Beware of false prophets who come to you in sheep's clothing, for inwardly they are ravening wolves.*

My brief informative session with 'butterfingers' or 'magician' or whatever he was meant that I would not have time to visit Whitehall and see St Barry's stone boat so I returned to the cruiser and we set out for our next port of call, Richmond Harbour in the village of Clondara. We left the lovely Termonbarry behind us, with its romantic tree-lined wharfs, and little gardens of gaily coloured flowers. A cruiser coming downstream had its short flagstaff snapped off by the low navigational arch on the bridge and I had a moment or two of anxiety as we sailed under and although we made it without striking, I imagine we had no more than a few inches to spare. Up river we kept close to the west bank as the east side is rocky and shoal, and soon we turned to starboard between the perches that mark the narrow entrance to the Camlin river. According to the prophecies of St Columcille, the Camlin river would run red with blood three times and after the third time the end of the world would come. This strange phenomenon has already happened twice. The first time was in 1798 after the Battle of Ballinamuck. Following the failure of the rising the English soldiers went on a frenzy of slaughter, dragged thousands of innocent men, women and children from their cabins and butchered them on the banks of the Camlin so that for weeks the river ran red with blood. The second occasion was more prosaic. During a great cholera epidemic in 1832, a Longford butcher killed hundreds of sheep to feed the starving population and the blood coloured the river for two days. The third occasion has not yet come.

The Camlin river is very narrow and weedy and we had to travel slowly and carefully lest the weeds fouled our propeller or choked our water-inlet. As we moved apprehensively along, we could almost touch the cattle grazing

102

on the marshy banks and we had some difficulty in restraining Maxie from jumping ashore to give chase. After nearly half-an-hour of this winding, tortuous, labyrinthine river we finally arrived at the tiny lock opening into Richmond Harbour. We had only a few minutes to wait for the friendly lock-keeper who put us quickly through and we berthed in one of the most romantic and poetic harbours on the entire River Shannon.

Richmond Harbour is a little paradise, a place of silence and peace. An old world tavern that has lost none of its time-honoured charm stands invitingly near the edge of the quay, flanked by venerable houses of a bygone age. The beauty of the little village is reflected in the friendliness of the people. In a shop where we made some purchases we asked for lettuce and rhubarb. They had none but the owner brought us out into the garden and invited us to take all the lettuce and rhubarb we wanted and refused to take any payment. While Mary and Gerald prepared dinner I strolled with Maxie across the picturesque bridge to the ruins of an old distillery. It once employed seventy men but when the great apostle of temperance, Father Matthew, swept across the country administering the pledge to hundreds of thousands of drunkards dwindling sales forced it to close down. Its old mill wheel now stands gaunt and rotting and the stream that powered it, choked with weeds. I rambled into the graveyard which was once the site of a monastery whose speciality was curing lunatics. It was said that every deranged person who spent an all-night vigil in the church would find himself cured in the morning. Only the ruins of the church, draped in a green net of ivy, now remain. What a great pity the tradition did not last. It would do a rip-roaring trade today. I wandered around through the ancient headstones, many bearded with moss, and could feel a gentle touch of holiness filling the air. The vespers of the old monks were now replaced by the evensong of the birds in the setting sun. I found one old headstone with a carving of a scissors and a head of hair which local tradition holds to be the grave of a family of hairdressers. Another headstone had the inscription:

> *Stay traveller stay.*
> *See where I lie*
> *As you are now so once was I*
> *As I am now so you shall be*
> *Prepare for death and follow me.*

Later I was told that a traveller who read these lines replied:

> *To follow you I am quite content*
> *But I am damned if I know*
> *The road you went*
> *So let me know where e'er you are*
> *And I'll go there, if it's not too far.*

Back on board we had dinner and later went to the hall to attend a session of *Siamsa*. This was a concert of Irish music, song and dance put on by a local group. It was a delight to look at; skilful Irish dancing, old ballads and songs grave and gay, recitations, sad and haunting melodies. It lasted for nearly two hours without a dull item. When it was over we strolled back at our ease to the boat, sat out on deck for a little while before going to bed, admiring this most idyllic haven, sensing the almost heavenly peace and tranquillity that enveloped this land-locked lagoon. The night was full of mystery. A shy moon peeped through the trees casting little streams of light across the still water, caressing the earth with a fairy happiness. The air was in the grip of an enchantment not of this world, motionless, eternal, infinite, frightening:

> *All things are hushed, as Nature's self lay dead;*
> *The mountains seemed to nod their drowsy head,*
> *And little birds in dreams their songs repeat,*
> *And sleeping flowers beneath the night-dew sweet;*
> *Even lust and envy sleep, yet love denies*
> *Rest to my soul and slumber to my eyes.*

5

Next morning I got up early and as I started out on a long walk with Maxie I remembered the comment of a simpleton I knew as a boy. 'There's nothing as early as morning,' he said. This comment was not without a grain of truth. There is a peace and tranquillity about early morning that seems to vanish by eight o'clock when humans bestir themselves. There is also an unspoiled freshness, a kind of exhilaration which seems to remind us that we are being given a chance to live another day. It rained lightly during the night and I heard the gentle patter on the cabin roof. As a child I was told that the raindrops were the angels' tears for a suffering world and in old age I have found no reason to doubt the wisdom of that allegory. It was a morning of indescribable beauty, fresh and sparkling, a morning that made one feel sixteen again on the very threshold of first love. The singing of the birds brought dreams of an orchestra playing Schubert's serenade; the mist still lingering along the banks had a kind of virginal purity about it; to my romantic dreaming mind it was like the first morning that God created paradise. I crossed the bridge and walked down the canal path under an archway of trees. The raindrops, like sparkling jewels, still clung to the leaves, and twinkled in the hearts of the flowers. The showers had awakened the warm green earth and the beauty of the summer morning was being echoed in the rich love-song of a blackbird. I passed the first lock; below it a few cruisers were moored to the bank. They had spent the night in these peaceful surroundings. They were surely continentals, I thought, for many of us Irish have not yet learned the beauty of solitude. I rambled along down the bank until I reached the broad expanse of the Shannon and then swung right by the edge of the water. The heat of the morning sun seemed to be soaking itself in the wet grass and tenderly drawing little whisps of steam up into the clear air. Walking along the banks of the Shannon on this beautiful morning I became a child again. I seemed to shake off the burden of the years, the formalism of daily living, the silly appearances to be kept up. I forgot the terrible mistakes of the past as if they never happened. The sadness and disappointments of life seemed to vanish into the swirling water and the far-off joys of youth returned again. The gifted writer, who created *Alice in Wonderland*, expressed that longing:

> *I'd give all wealth that toil hath piled*
> *The bitter fruit of life's decay*
> *To be once more a little child*
> *For one short summer's day.*

Maxie was having the time of his life chasing water-hens and other wild fowl who evaded him by simply swimming out into the river and remaining stationary. He gazed after them with a puzzled angry look, but took good care not to venture beyond his depth. I walked on and on until I was nearly at the Termonbarry weir, and then swung around again, until I eventually reached the main Clondara road. I had been walking for nearly two hours and had not seen a soul. As I enjoyed the beauty of that walk it was easy to understand how the magnificence of the earth inspired the poets:

> *I am glad when morning and evening alter the skies*
> *There speaks no voice of the stars but my voice replies;*
> *When wave on wave all night cries out its need*
> *I listen, I understand, my heart takes heed.*
>
> *Out of the red-brown earth, out of the grey-brown streams*
> *Came this perilous body, cage of perilous dreams;*
> *To the ends of all waters and lands, they are tossed,*
> *   They are whirled*
> *For my dreams all one with my body, yea one with the*
> *   world.*

After breakfast we left Richmond Harbour and wound our way slowly back down the Camlin river. I do not believe I will ever travel this river as long as it remains in its present state. It is far too weedy and one is continually on edge wondering if the propeller will get fouled. The Camlin river opens out into the beautiful Lough Forbes with its luxuriant wooded shores on one side, contrasting with the barren grasslands, like a badly shaven head, on the other. The reason is, of course, that the wooded shore on the east was planted centuries ago by the earls of Granard. Although the Castle Forbes estate was the scene of many bitter encounters in the last century, when the tenants refused to pay the exhorbitant rents demanded of them, on the whole the Granards were considered fair landlords. Inside the walls and behind the castle itself there is the remains of a graveyard in which, prior to the year 1800, the people of the parish had permission to bury their dead. But the then Earl of Granard did not wish the Irish to be crossing his demesne, so he closed the graveyard to everyone except members of his own family. This angered the people very much as the tradition of being buried in one's family grave is deep rooted. But an Irishman always finds a way and so they buried their dead at night when the earl was asleep. However, when he found out what was going on he had the graveyard examined each morning and if any fresh grave were found he would have his workmen disinter the corpse and throw it out on the side of the road. At that time there was a well known fighter living in the village who went by the name of 'Bullawatha'. When he was dying he asked his sons to bury him with his father and mother in the forbidden burial ground. 'Put a good blackthorn stick at my right hand in the coffin,' he said. 'For you'd never know when I'd find use for it.' Soon afterwards he died and they carried out his request. But the Earl of Granard heard of the burial and had the corpse forthwith flung on the side of the road. Next morning the earl was found dead in bed. His death was caused, they say, by a blow from a heavy stick on the head.

I had heard a lot of complaints about our next port of call, Roosky; that it was a cowboy town, that people were unfriendly and given to over-charging, so when we arrived there my mind was slightly hostile. I do not know how it got that name. I found it clean and tidy, well laid out and we were charged no more for what we bought there than we were charged anywhere else. The few contacts I had with the people I found them helpful and friendly. Like Termonbarry the wharfs are beautifully situated on a tree-lined avenue. We made fast to one of them, had a cup of coffee and strolled around the village for an hour or so. There was a great deal of trouble in Roosky in the early part of the nineteenth century. It was here one of the first strikes in the history of modern industrial relations took place. The men who were working on the construction of the bridge and lock went on strike for higher wages, but according to a contemporary account the 'magistrates and constabulary soon restored order'. On another occasion the government erected a wickerwood weir in order to trap eels and thus take away the livelihood of many fishermen. But everytime it was erected it was pulled down so in the end the government faced the inevitable and let things be. After Roosky we called to the tiny harbour at Dromod and strolled around the well-ordered village and visited a delightful shop where one can buy everything from the proverbial needle to anchor. This is a lovely little harbour, another of the Shannon's secret places, an old resting spot for the barges of long ago. It was built in 1829 for the sum of £139. A new and enlarged harbour is now under construction.

We retraced our course and sailed on into the picturesque Lough Bofin with its beautifully wooded shoreline. As we passed through the narrow channel by Derrycarne Wood my mind jumped across the centuries to the old ninth century monk who heard a blackbird singing somewhere in the trees and gave expression to his joy in a simple poem:

Oh blackbird of Derrycarne wood
Piping in your leafy nest
No melody in all the earth
Could be for me more welcome guest.

Oh Patrick of the heavenly bells
If you could hear this faultless air
You'd rise up from your sombre tomb
And once more chant the sunset prayer.

Derrycarne, once forbidden to the Irish, is now a national park where every citizen of the land can enjoy its many beauties. We crossed Lough Boderg, which got its name from a red cow presented to the local people by a mermaid whom they befriended, and entered the beautiful Carnadoe waters. The passage to Grange is quite complicated, but it has the saving grace that if you make a mistake nothing very serious can happen. Nearly all the navigation marks have been renewed by *The Silver Eel Restaurant* at Grange and without their enterprise it would be quite difficult to find one's way. We stayed a short half hour at Grange itself, where there is really only bank mooring, and returned again to our course. The beauty of the Carnadoe waters is almost primeval. I cannot imagine that it has changed much over the past few thousand years. It is a place where the gentleness of heaven creeps over the earth, where all care and troubles sleep. Reed beds, little islands enfolded by the arms of the bays, wild rugged shoreline, peace and tranquillity, all give you the feeling that you are in another world. But it is not a place for cruisers; rather it is a place for the fisherman, the philosopher in his rowing boat, or the patient bird-watcher ever seeking new species, or indeed the honeymoon couple lost in the lilac days of love, dreaming dreams all too soon to turn into hard realities. The cruiser is really out of place in these waters of unearthly beauty. We sailed through the pleasant Lough Tap and then up a particularly attractive stretch of river to the little harbour at Drumsna where we had lunch. Drumsna, where Anthony Trollope worked in the post office and wrote *The Mac-*

Dermots of Ballycloran, is a very pleasant village with a good restaurant, excellent shops, one of which looked particularly attractive with its artistic woodcarvings. After lunch we retraced our course again and turned to starboard into the Jamestown Canal. We tied up at the wharf below Albert Lock and I rambled up to renew acquaintanceship with Mattie Bourke. Mattie has been described by one newspaper as 'the king of the lock-keepers' and that was quite an apt description for he is every inch a king. Intelligent, dignified and wise, with a delightful roughish sense of humour, he is a friend to everyone boating on the Shannon. For many years his health has not been too good, but his unconquerable spirit has enabled him to carry on with a smile and a good word for all. We chatted for about half-an-hour while the lock was being cleared, exchanged stories and Shannon lore, and as I was going back to the boat he gave me a present of a bunch of rhubarb from his colourful rustic garden. Through the lock we entered the Jamestown Canal, which is a minor masterpiece of engineering, cut out of sheer rock. The story is told that when the canal was being constructed in the last century, a number of bronze objects of great archaeological interest were found and a special reward paid to the workmen who dug them up. With such encouragement it is no wonder that the diligent labourers kept a sharp eye out and the result was that great hoards of these valuable objects were brought to light. The museum authorities were very excited by these finds and they came down on a special mission hoping to find perhaps a hidden city. On closer examination it turned out that a local blacksmith was working hammer-and-tongs manufacturing them and sharing the proceeds with the navvies. It is said that the experts were unable to distinguish the real from the false so no prosecution was initiated. As we went through the canal we were persecuted by horse flies who gave us many nasty stings before we got rid of them. Back again in the Shannon we turned to starboard and tied up at the homely wharf near Jamestown Bridge. I strolled along the tree-lined road into the village which was taken

110

from the O'Rourkes and handed over to planters by James I, who had the place called after himself. Across the road from me I could see the meagre remains of the fortifications which Patrick Sarsfield levelled to the ground. There is something else which might usefully be levelled too, two old pillars which are a really serious traffic hazard, and are of no particular archaeological interest. I went into the Catholic church and was intrigued to find a ledger giving the amount of dues paid by the parishioners at Christmas and Easter. This ledger was in a public place so that everyone could see it and from the amounts paid one could make his own judgment on the standing of the various families. I rambled through the historic old graveyard where there is a plaque erected to commemorate the excommunication of the Marquis of Ormond in 1650. I do not know of anywhere else in the world where there is a public memorial to a man being kicked out of the Church. Back again on board we had a quick cup of coffee and started on the last lap of our journey for that day.

Although the trip from Jamestown to Carrick is short, the scenery is delightful. There is a modest loveliness about the river here as it winds its way through the soft tranquillity of Lough Corry, alive with moor-hens, cootes, herons and grebe splashing with joy in the freshness of the water. As we sailed along a soft south westerly breeze reinvigorated the sultry summer's day and as the evening sun began to drop behind the Curlew Mountains we arrived at Carrick-on-Shannon and tied up at a well laid-out, well serviced jetty belonging to one of the hire companies. In a sense Carrick is the capital of the Shannon waterway. Three major hire companies with a combined fleet of hundreds of cruisers are located here, as well as many clubs plying with all kinds of water pastimes. It is the Baltimore of the inland waterways. I went ashore and called in to the offices of *Carrick Craft* to pay my respects. I once hired a cruiser of their magnificent Mayo class and both my companions and myself were profoundly impressed by the efficiency and courtesy which characterised all their dealings with us. Prior

111

to taking over the cruiser the manager, Mr G. F. Lothian, in a delightfully persuasive accent, gave us a most informative lecture and demonstration, using models, on the operation of the engine, and on the handling of craft in the water. This was followed by a practical lesson on the river and it was all so well done that even the most inexperienced novice found the handling of a boat a matter of simplicity. His assistant, Mr A. Kelly, saw to it that all our material comforts on board were up to the highest standards and no request, however foolish, dimmed his unfailing courtesy.

We decided to take a rest from cooking so we strolled up the town to the famous Bush Hotel. The Bush is a hotel which never lost its character. It has not succumbed to the terrible cult of clinical chromium plate and meaningless works of art which has destroyed so many otherwise good hotels. On its walls hang elegant, graceful paintings and one of the things we specially admired was the priceless collection of old Shannon prints decorating the passage to the dinning-room. I was also glad to see a stand of Irish paperbacks in the hall and once again I was told that these Irish books outsell all others. Seemingly, the tourist who comes to Ireland wants above all to read about Ireland, its history, its people, its culture and especially its humour. After a most relishable dinner we strolled lazily around the town doing a little window shopping. Like most of the towns on the Shannon the shops are exceptionally well stocked. In one of them, which was open, we made a lot of purchases and the owner would not hear of us carrying two large cardboard boxes of groceries with us. Instead he had them delivered almost immediately to our boat. We called in to see what is reputed to be the smallest church in the world, which contains the two leaden coffins of a man and his wife united forever in death. On our way back we ran into Mr John Conway of *Emerald Star Lines*, one of the largest and best hire companies. In their reception room they have an excellent stand of Irish paperbacks and John confirmed what I had already heard, that all foreign tourists avidly read books about Ireland. I decided to have an early night but as so often happens on the Shannon 'the best laid plans of mice and men gang aft agley'. I met an attractive, petite, good-looking girl whom I knew, and who was also cruising with her parents. She very kindly invited me on board their boat for one 'very tiny, tiny nightcap'. We were later joined by two highly intelligent friends of hers with a magnificent repertoire of stories. As one tale borrowed another, and as the outbursts of laughter increased, so too did the size of the 'nightcaps', and many hours later I picked my steps, with some uncertainty I admit, back to our cruiser and bed.

Early next day we left Carrick for Leitrim village, which is only a short distance away. The morning mist was still haunting the banks of the river, but the sunshine was breaking through and beginning to warm the earth. We made our way through the narrow wandering river, its banks tapestried with green, until we finally tied up at the wharf below Leitrim Bridge. This small village is steeped in history. It was from here the tragic Dervorgilla left her cruel husband and eloped with Dermot MacMurrogh. This is all O'Rourke country and in the sixteenth century one of the O'Rourkes, to show his contempt for Queen Elizabeth, tied an effigy of her to his horse's tail He was later arrested and executed in London for this act. He refused to recognised the court or ask for mercy. His only request was that he be hanged with a halter made of withy, which was used to hang Irish peasants, rather than with English hemp. His son Brian O'Rourke was taken by the English while still a child, and educated at Oxford, Hampton and Middle Temple. When it was thought he was a young English gentleman he was asked to return to Ireland and influence his clan to give allegiance to the British crown. The proud youth refused and so was imprisoned in the Tower of London where he died thirty years later. The O'Rourkes were ultimately driven from their lands and they fled to the continent. In modern times one of them became Bishop of Danzig. He was forced to leave that city when it was occupied by the Nazis and it was reported later that he was murdered by the Russians. Leitrim was also the final home of the great

113

O'Sullivan Bere after his long winter march from Cork. He left with one thousand souls and when he arrived here only thirty-five were still alive.

We managed to get a car in the village to take us a few miles to the little hillside graveyard of Kilronan, overlooking the wooded shores of Lough Meelagh just outside Keadue, where the remains of the greatest of Irish composers, the blind Turlough Carolan, were laid to rest. We climbed through the lines of headstones to a holy solitude at the top, to the vault of the MacDermotroe family where this brilliant composer is buried. The MacDermotroes were his patrons and it was their help made it possible for him to devote so much time to his music. Carolan lost his sight when he was sixteen years of age, but as he said himself, his ears took the place of his eyes. He was a composer of the people. His dreams were those of the common man. His haunting melodies expressed all the tragedy, sorrow and love of a suffering race. Shortly before he died he took his harp and with trembling feeble fingers composed his most famous piece: *Farewell to Music*. He never played again. Sadly he drank too much. On his death bed he was unable to swallow. He asked those around him to put his favourite tankard to his lips, 'for,' he said, 'two such old companions should not part without a farewell kiss.' These were his last words. When he died his wake lasted four full days and it is said that upwards of one thousand people were blind drunk during the entire mourning period. Some time later his skull was dug up and placed in a niche in the wall where it was venerated until it was stolen by a lightfingered tourist.

It is impossible to stand by his grave unmoved. You can almost hear the faint chords of his sad music living far beyond the world he left so tragically:

> *Kilronan Abbey is his castle now*
> *And there 'till dooms-day peacefully he'll stay*
> *In vain they weave new garlands for his brow*
> *In vain they go to meet him by the way*
> *In kindred company he does not tire*

The native dead and noble lie around
His life-long song has ceased, his wood and wire
Rest, a sweet harp unstrung, in holy ground.

Back again on the boat we returned and sailed up the Boyle river towards our final destination, Lough Key. The sheer beauty of these waters is almost beyond description. The banks were embroidered with multi-coloured trees, their branches like locks of curly hair; the corn in the fields was bending to the soft wind scampering across the landscape; here and there clusters of thirsty flowers drooped their heads to touch the sparkling water; amongst the hedges long fingers of wild honeysuckle spread gusts of exquisite perfume through the air; nets of mystical summer haze enfolded the rolling hills. The whole journey, through the crystal clear Drumharlow lake, dominated by the fairy hills Sheebeg and Sheemore, past the little village of Cootehall, was a sheer delight to body and soul.

A little wayside lake asleep
Can catch the eyes of stars that peep.

The frailest flower that decks the sod
Reflects the glory of its God.

The flowing stream of Time can be
A shadow of Eternity.

But where, O Lady, shall I find
A mystic lamp to guide the mind?

I wanted to stop at every bend, to linger silently among the blossom-laden banks, and like Horace, think such thoughts as are worthy of a wise man. But time was against us and we continued on, slowly, until we reached the wharf below Knockvickar Lock. Here the silence was only broken by the melodious sound of the waterfall, the lowing of cows, the cry of a frightened bird, the distant bleating of sheep. A solitary lark, like a speck in the sky, mingled the notes of her song with the music of the earth. This is my favourite spot on the river. It is a place to refresh the mind and to banish the cobwebs of the soul. While Mary and Gerald were preparing lunch, I strolled along a beautiful rural pathway of arched trees towards the village itself. All along the grassy margin little daisies tossed their heads, sleepy bees seemed to doze among the fuschia bells, known to the people as the tears of God. Maxie had the time of his life chasing butterflies, insects and birds. I walked to the bridge and back, a hushed observer of the poetry of the river, of the great beauty which draws us into commune with that which lies beyond all beauty, the mysterious eternal. It is said that St Columcille and his monks were walking along this path one day when they came across a bard with his harp, sitting across from the weir. They asked him to play and sing for them, but he refused on the grounds that he was in mourning for his wife. Then St Columcille waved his crozier and the bard's wife came back from the dead and stood before them. Instead of being happy to be alive again she launched out in an abusive attack on her husband because, she said, he should have given her a more elaborate and expensive funeral. Whereupon St Columcille waved his crozier again and the wife was swept back into the grave once more. The bard realising that a nod is as good as a wink took up his harp and played some of the sweetest music and sang the loveliest songs for Columcille and the monks and kept this up until they were well out of sight.

After lunch we reluctantly left this little paradise and went into the lock. John Coggin, who has a smile and a friendly word for everyone, put us quickly through. 'The weather is rising,' he said as he bade us farewell. 'Ye'll have a good day on the lake.' Just beyond the lock we entered the beautiful Lough Key. John was right. Summer was spilling its joy all over the lake and its myriad of little wooded islands that looked as if they were only anchored to the bottom and might move at any time. It is said that about 3,500 BC, there was a rumbling all over Roscommon and Sligo and nine lakes suddenly appeared, one of which was Lough Key. Instead of going straight to Rockingham, I set course for Trinity Island, which I wanted to visit. W. B. Yeats, in one of his mystical periods, tried to start a

116

commune of writers, artists and philosophers on this island, but the project came to nothing. I wanted to visit the island to see two graves, that of Sir Conyers Clifford, and the grave of Una MacDermot and Tomás Costello. Sir Conyers was the English general who was defeated by Red Hugh O'Donnell at the famous battle of the nearby Curlew Mountains. Clifford's army was routed and he himself was beheaded in the fight. Some of his retainers sent a request to MacDermot, O'Donnell's field commander, to return Clifford's body so that they might give it a decent burial. MacDermot chivalrously agreed. He sent the body to Trinity Island for burial although he could not find the head. 'Take good care,' he instructed his couriers, 'that you wrap the general in a clean linen sheet.' They were decent men in those days. But the grave I wanted to see most was of Una MacDermot and Tomás Costello. Una was the beautiful daughter of the local chieftain MacDermot who lived on Castle Island. She fell deeply in love with Tomás, but her father thought her much too good for him and he put an abrupt stop to their courtship. Una became suddenly ill and, despite the best medical care at the time, she got worse and worse. Tomás made one last desperate attempt to soften her father, but the old man refused even to see him. He waited on horseback knee deep in the River Boyle for several hours hoping that MacDermot would relent, but it was all to no avail and he rode away broken hearted. A few hours later Una died. She was buried on Trinity Island, or Abbey Island as it was then called. Every evening for a fortnight Tomás swam across the lake and spent the night by Una's grave. Then one morning a shepherd found him stretched across the mound of earth, dead. Only then did old MacDermot yield and agreed to allow Tomás to be buried with the girl he loved. Local tradition says they found on his body the manuscript of a love song he wrote for Una, one of the most tender and haunting love songs in the Irish language. *Una Bhain* is untranslatable except in spirit:

My Una of the ringletted shimmering hair
Like a candle of gold gracing the royal fare
Like a garden rose kissed by the morning dew
I'd curse my God, I'd damn my soul for you.

My Una of the golden wind-tossed hair
The cold grave holds you now, so young, so fair
Your graceful body that was my love's dream
Decays like flotsam on a weed-choked stream.

I waited for you in the waters cold
My hungry eyes sought out your head of gold
I waited 'till the stars came one by one
I waited 'till the last of day was done.

And then I crossed the stream and went my way
And wandered frenzied 'till the newborn day
Lost in the woods, indifferent to my fate
Cursing your father − curses scourged with hate.

A horseman came and told me how you cried
And told me that at break of day you died
The Abbey isle shall now become my 'stead
Your nameless lonely grave our bridal bed.

There was not enough water at the little jetty to go along-side so we prudently anchored off and went ashore in the punt. When we landed we were overwhelmed by a melancholic sense of tragedy. The entire island, outside the monastic ruins, was covered with weeds, briars, ferns and bushes up to four feet high. We had to cut our way through this dense undergrowth with sticks, but although we searched for nearly an hour we could not find a trace of any grave. Disappointed we returned on board and as we sailed away I thought of how neglectful we are of some of our greatest antiquities. Every year thousands of people visit the grave of Romeo and Juliet in Verona, yet here the only mementoes we have of the Irish Romeo and Juliet are weeds and nettles.

We skirted around Drummane Island and tied up at the wharf near Rockingham Pier. This hugh estate now belongs to the Irish nation. It once belonged to the Irish chieftains, MacDermot, but it was taken from them and given to a planter family who for a long time brutally treated their tenants, and literally splashed the estate with the blood of the Irish. In the earlier part of the last century the Rockingham landlords had the reputation of being amongst the cruellest in the whole country. I could never imagine how they could live in such a place and be so cruel, for the beauty of Lough Key could only soften the heart and inspire one to love the goodness of life. Today you can still see the vast maze of dark tunnels constructed so that the comings and goings of the Irish workers would not spoil the view of their betters. As one contemporary historian said, 'there is thus no appearance of menial movement near the house.' At the end of one of these tunnels was a bench where the tenants paid their rents. Sometimes they were left there in the cold for days, and if they attempted to go home they were evicted from their lands. One of the severest punishments handed out in those far-off days to the disobedient was to carry paniers of manure on their shoulders all day long until the weight cut into their shoulders and the dirt burned into their flesh. Then they were manacled and chained for the night. Local tradition tells how the Irish, when they were emigrating, used to bathe their wrists in a kind of goat's buttermilk to obliterate the marks of the chains. Stories are still told of how in those terrible days of the middle of the last century, the lord of the manor forced the good-looking daughters of the tenants to attend to the needs of the visiting gentry after dinner parties. One such young girl who refused was dragged by her hair behind a horse until she was dead. When her brothers protested they were mysteriously drowned in Lough Key and her father and mother evicted. An old man who lived in the area once told me what he had heard about them when he was a child. 'More than a hundred years ago a lot of the landlords around here had their tenants' houses built with no back door so that when his lordship called in a randy mood the daughter couldn't escape out the back.

119

Then after a drunken dinner party the gamekeeper would fire a shot in the yard and that was a sign for six or eight tenants' daughters to move into the bedrooms and strip off to their pelts and if they refused their families would be evicted. One of the worst of these landlords was in Rockingham just before the great famine. He was a randy ould bastard who was always chasing the tenants' daughters and I heard my great-grandfather to say that this lord was so randy that whenever he saw a good-looking girl you could hear his balls rattling nearly as far away as Boyle. But all them bad times changed at the end of the century when the tenants got their rights and couldn't be evicted at the whim of a landlord. Anyway that's all past and gone, and the later owners were decent people who looked after their tenants.'

The sun shone brilliantly on this late summer afternoon. We went ashore and rambled through the park. Everywhere people were walking around, the children playing and the old dozing in the shade. It was great to think that this beautiful park now belonged to them and I wondered if any spared a thought for their ancestors whose sacrifices, sufferings and indomitable courage made all this possible. We looked first at the ruins of the great mansion, then the ice house and then on to the old church rebuilt in 1833 by one of the lords with a roving eye. After that we strolled along through an arboretum where almost every kind of tree grew, then along an avenue of red cedars, over a rustic bridge on to Drummane Island, through a forest and on to the amazing Bog Gardens ablaze with azalea and rhododendron. We wandered along through all kinds of byways and pathways and finally returned to the boat three hours later tired and hungry. When we were having dinner on deck, the sun began to set in a burning sea of gold and the last crimson waves of light gave way to the creeping darkness. We sat chatting until the first cool breeze of night rippled over the water and the early stars began to wink and twinkle in the sky. Gerald and Mary went to bed, but I sat out for a while longer in a pensive mood, my restless thoughts, each one contradicting the other. I let the mood of the moment drift aimlessly through my mind. Twilight has a strange effect upon the human being. It may be the hour when young lovers whisper tender words of hope and trust, but for others, no so young, twilight can be tinged with sadness and with premonitions of an eternity around the corner. Here I remembered Ledwidge's haunting poem on *Growing Old.*

> *We'll fill a province bowl and pledge us deep*
> *The memory of far ones, and between*
> *The soothing pipes, in heavy-lidded sleep,*
> *Perhaps we'll dream the things that once have been.*
> *'Tis only noon and still too soon to die*
> *Yet we are growing old, my heart and I*
>
> *A hundred books are ready in my head*
> *To open out where Beauty bent a leaf.*
> *What do we want with Beauty? We are wed*
> *Like ancient Prosperine to dismal grief.*
> *And we are changing with the hours that fly,*
> *And growing odd and old, my heart and I.*
>
> *Across a bed of bells the river flows,*
> *And roses dawn, but not for us; we want*
> *The new thing ever as the old thing grows*
> *Spectral and weary on the hills we haunt.*
> *And that is why we feast, and that is why*
> *We're growing odd and old, my heart and I.*

There is a sadness behind all beauty — there has to be in a world where everything we love must die. But tonight I refused to let those sad thoughts occupy my mind. Instead I remembered there is always Hope, which, next to Love, is the greatest of Christian virtues. It helps to come to grips with the perplexing uncertainties of the future, with the imponderable questions of life, suffering and death to which there is no rational answer available to the mind of man. Hamlet's terrifying question *to be or not to be* remains unsolved throughout the centuries, but in spite of that the words of the psalmist bring some consolation:

God will wipe away all tears from their eyes;
There will be no more death and no more mourning or
  sadness
The world of the past has gone.

Well, our cruise is over. Soon we will drive back to the city, to the realities of everyday living; to strikes, muggings, robberies, income tax, balance sheets, energy crises and all the turmoil we had forgotten on the river. The end of our little holiday has come, as there is an end to everything beautiful in this world, even an end to life itself; well, not really everything. The magic of the Shannon which has lasted from the dawn of history will live on after all of us have made our final harbour, on and on through the aeons of time until the final moment of eternity.

When the birds had sung the last of their twilight melodies and everything was silent I slowly made my way to bed.

God, who lights the little stars,
And over night the white dew spills;
Whose hand doth move the season's cars
And clouds that mock our pointed hills;
Whose bounty fills the cow-trod wold,
And fills with bread the warm brown sod;
Who brings us sleep, where we grow old
'Til sleep and age together nod;
Reach out a beam and touch the pain
A heart has oozed through all the years
Your pity dries the morning tears
And fills the world with joy again.

MORE INTERESTING BOOKS

THE SECRET PLACES
OF THE
BURREN

JOHN M. FEEHAN

John M. Feehan searches out the hidden corners of the Burren, those secluded places where time stands still and where nature speaks its secret language to the human spirit.

Although at times controversial, cutting through sham and pretence wherever he meets it, he writes with great charm, skill and sympathy, and with a deep love of the countryside and its people.

He sees the mystery, the beauty and the sense of wonder in ordinary things and brings each situation to life so that the reader feels almost physically present.

This is a most delightful Irish travel book that can be read again and again.

THE SECRET PLACES
OF THE
WEST CORK
COAST

JOHN M. FEEHAN

Cork, the largest county in Ireland, has hundreds of miles of indented coastline, which is regarded as one of the scenic jewels of the country. John M. Feehan sailed alone in a small boat around the West Cork coast in search of true peace, his 'land of the heart's desire', his 'isle of the blest'.

The result is a book that is not only a profound spiritual odyssey but a magnificent account of the wild rugged coastline, the peaceful coves and the unique characters he met in this beautiful, unspoiled corner of Ireland.

John M. Feehan writes with great charm, skill and sympathy, and with a mischievous roguish humour, often at his own expense. His sharp eye misses nothing. He sees the mystery, beauty and wonder in ordinary things, and brings situations and people vividly to life.

MY VILLAGE
MY WORLD

JOHN M. FEEHAN

*This is a book that never palls or drags. It is boisterous and rib-
ald and I am tempted to say that it is by far the funniest book I
have ever read. It is also an accurate and revealing history of
rural Ireland half a century ago and more. John M. Feehan writes
beautifully throughout. I love this book.*

From the Freword by JOHN B. KEANE

My Village – My World is a fascinating account of ordinary
people in the countryside. It depicts a way of life that took
thousands of years to evolve and mature and was destroyed in
a single generation. As John M. Feehan says 'Nobody famous
ever came from our village. None of its inhabitants ever
achieved great public acclaim ... The people of our village could
be described in government statistics as unskilled. That would
be a false de-scription. They were all highly skilled, whether in
constructing privies or making coffins, digging drains or cutting hedges, droving cattle or tending to stallions ... I do not
want to paint a picture of an idyllic village like Goldsmith's
phony one. We had our sinners as well as our saints ...'

THE SHOOTING OF MICHAEL COLLINS
MURDER OR ACCIDENT?

JOHN M. FEEHAN

Was Michael Collins killed by accident of war or was he ruthlessly murdered? Both of these possibilities are calmly and carefully examined by the author, who has rejected the traditional theory that he was killed as a result of a ricochet rifle bullet and leans towards the possibility that he was shot by a Mauser pistol.

When the first and second editions of this book appeared they sold out instantly and caused a newspaper controversy which lasted many months. This new updated and rewritten edition, incorporating new and rather startling information, is sure to arouse exceptional and absorbing interest in this baffling and bewildering mystery.